LAMENT
OF AN EXPAT

LAMENT
OF AN EXPAT

How I Discovered America
And Tried to Mend It.

LEONORA BURTON

authorHOUSE®

AuthorHouse™
1663 Liberty Drive
Bloomington, IN 47403
www.authorhouse.com
Phone: 1-800-839-8640

Published by AuthorHouse   04/01/2013

ISBN: 978-1-4817-3371-7 (sc)
ISBN: 978-1-4817-3370-0 (hc)
ISBN: 978-1-4817-3369-4 (e)

Library of Congress Control Number: 2013905503

Front Cover Design: Jane Marcy
Front Cover Picture: Credit NY Daily News
Back Cover Picture: Jane Marcy

To my researcher, the ghostly Tony, who haunts these pages

Any errors in this book could not possibly be my fault.

CHAPTER ONE

My first close encounter with democracy American-style and, I suppose, to some extent American capitalism, came some weeks after I arrived in Manhattan from England. I found myself jumping up and down while shouting lustily at presidential candidate Richard M. Nixon. I should add that it was not in anger but in pursuit of the holy dollar.

At this point I had installed myself in an East Side apartment and, having nearly overcome a fear that every cab driver in town had been instructed to run me over whenever I appeared on the streets, I was beginning to feel a bit like a New Yorker, albeit a slightly disaffected one. A neighbor accosted me one day as I was opening my apartment door and asked if I would like to make a few dollars, in fact 25 of them, which in those days was worth my attention. What would I have to do?

I would have to put on a red, white and blue dress and a straw boater she supplied and report to a midtown hotel where Nixon had a campaign engagement. In England the candidate was hardly a household name but I had picked up enough to conclude he was a politician of the Republican persuasion. When I got there I discovered there was a group of young women similarly garbed. One of Nixon's henchmen instructed us that we were "volunteers", better not mention any payment. Now we were "Nixon Girls" and when he appeared we should wave our boaters, jump up and down and scream "Nixon's the one!"

We giggled and arranged ourselves as ordered, although I thought I heard one girl mutter that she was a goddamned Democrat and it went against her principles. Apparently her principles were undermined by a handful of dollars. Capitalism at work. In accents I was just getting used to they said Mr. Nixon had been nicknamed "Tricky Dicky". Joining in the spirit of it, I offered another one, "Wretched Richard," but they decided they preferred "Tricky Dicky". Shortly afterwards, the man himself appeared. He wore a dark suit, white shirt and subdued tie. His shoes were as glossy as a gigolo's. He looked as if he never wore anything but a suit and tie and went to bed in them. To imaginative me, he looked a tad constipated. As we went into our act, he gave an uneasy grin for the benefit of a gaggle of photographers who were lighting the corridor with their flashbulbs.

Members of the hovering press were invited to interview us. One reporter noted my accent and asked, "What are you doing at a Nixon rally?"

In a mischievous mood, I declared, "Oh, I'm so full of admiration for Mr. Nixon, I flew over from England especially to support him as he fights for the White House and the free world." The reporter looked skeptical—probably a Democrat—but scribbled it down in his notebook. Well, I doubt it was the first time political types had lied to the press, certainly not the last. And I was giving full value for my 25 dollars.

The next day our picture appeared on the front page of the Daily News. Of course. The scene was not for the benefit of bemused hotel guests but for the cameras. My goodness, look how popular Dick Nixon is in Democratic New York. On a succeeding night, in different dresses we did the same act at Madison Square Garden amid raucous hoopla. Nixon definitely was the one. We were allowed to keep the dresses. Much later I learned that the ineffable Roger Ailes, the Merlin who had conjured up Fox News from the deep, was orchestrating the Nixon campaign with his eerie genius for playing pinball in the skulls of his simple-minded targets. Maybe the Nixon Girls were the idea of the wily right wing ringmaster. With my energetic imagination, I could hear him instructing a flunky: "Get a bunch of bimbos and have them jumping up and down with excitement around Nixon. Gotta pretend he's a regular human being and not an automaton from outer space." Maybe shortly after arriving in New York I had become—horrors!—an Ailes Bimbo as well as a Nixon Girl. Years later I ran afoul of Ailes, by then the top earner for Rupert Murdoch, when he decided I was not an acolyte or even a supporter and therefore lurked in one of the many enemy camps surrounding him. Dear paranoid Roger, what a scamp, but we'll get to that.

Did I in my little way help Nixon win the 1968 election? Doubtful . . . in spite of my green card I couldn't even vote. In the U.K., it seemed to me, just about anybody resident in the country and still breathing could register and vote, not that very many wanted to.

I was not entirely new to the bizarre, nonsensical political game. When I was a teenager, my father stood (not ran) for election to the town council in Newport, Wales, where I was born, and I did my little bit. To help him ascend to the political heights my three older sisters and I were cornered by my dad and instructed to go knock on doors in the neighborhood and order residents to vote for Mr. James Fairclough (actually Jim to voters) while thrusting his campaign literature at them. My sister Sally, a tough cookie, flat-out refused to take part on the grounds that she didn't agree with his right wing political philosophy. They didn't get on. Sally was a twin whose brother did not survive the rigors of birth and she always felt that our father resented her for being alive instead of her lost twin brother. Hell, fate should have given him a male to help protect him from the monstrous regiment of women surrounding him. It may be that as she grew up he softened his attitude towards her for when she got married he walked her down the aisle.

Sally, mother of four, is now the mistress of a jewel of a country manor house overlooking the Bristol Channel and surrounded by hundreds of acres of land with the requisite his-and-her Mercedes saloons outside the barn and a couple of yellow Labradors. I suspect her politics have veered to the right.

Unlike Newport, Rhode Island, with its absurd shoulder-to-shoulder, look-at-me mansions, Newport, South Wales, was a working town, first as a port and then as a manufacturer of steel. Later, after the steel mills closed, it went high-tech and called itself the Welsh Seattle although nobody else did. It wasn't a pretty town and it was rained on a lot more than the American version.

At the time of the Newport election, I was on holiday from my boarding school in England where I was more interested in sports and boys (barred from the virginal precincts) than in politics or academics. Bothering neighbors seemed like a lot of fun so off I went.

The pleasure of interrupting lunch, dinner or who-knows-what quickly wore off. Indeed it became boring, especially when it rained, and soon I ditched the remaining literature in a bin and went to the pictures. On the streets afterwards we would encounter people who, depending on their political views, would say things like "Oh, there are the Fairclough girls, aren't they sweet?" or alternatively they would give us black scowls as if we carried the plague and stalk off.

When all four girls were at home on school vacations, father would insist that we go to Sunday services at the church around the corner, although he would not attend. We would sit at the very back row, ready to escape at the earliest opportunity. The vicar, known in the Welsh idiom as Charlie the Church, liked to enter from the rear. He would walk behind us, tickling us as he passed, so that we erupted in protests and giggles. Heading for the altar, he would declare to the congregation that the noise had nothing to do with him and that everybody should be appropriately quiet.

Charlie the Church forgave my father for his non-attendance because after giving his parishioners their weekly dose of religion he would drop round at our home, knowing that a dose of restorative gin awaited him.

From a certain angle my father, wiry and always busy, had slightly asymmetrical features because during the war he had tackled an unexploded incendiary bomb which suddenly went off making a mess of his face. Surgeons, used to the devastation of the blitz, skillfully repaired most of the damage by taking skin from his backside and using it to mask the wounds. The eventual result was that his features sported very smooth and soft skin for a middle aged man but it must have been uncomfortable for the patient to sit down for a while. That was the story told to me by my mother.

Another, this from my sisters, was that as a major in the Home Guard he was dismantling coastal defenses at the end of the war. These defenses included incendiary booby traps arranged to repel the brutish invaders. But in the course of his efforts one of these phosphorous bomblets blew up in his face. His men tried to take him to a hospital but he refused, said he just wanted to go home. He, of course, won the argument and appeared on my granny's doorstep, his face blackened and distorted like a creature from the black lagoon. This story has it that the horrified females of the family spent days, if not weeks, picking bits of metal out of his face until he regained something like normality. I don't know which story is more unlikely—often the case with my aberrant family—but my mother said that when as a toddler I first saw him, his head covered with bandages, I screamed and ran in terror, probably traumatized for life which would explain my peculiarities.

The more unfortunate result of his experience, whichever true, was that he developed diabetes and that meant he was strictly forbidden alcohol. At the age of about 9 or 10, I quite rightly took the alcohol ban extremely seriously and feared that the demon drink could do away with my strange father who, after all, was the only one I had. So it was that one evening I spotted him emerging from his study. Seeing me, he hid something behind his back. My suspicions were confirmed when I peeked behind him, and, yes, there it was, a glass of whiskey.

In a fine example of childish outrage, I darted around, lashed out and knocked the glass from his grip. The glass and alcohol went flying. I could see that he was not happy but I was old enough to recognize that attack was the best form of defense.

"What the hell d'you think you're . . ."

"Father," I said sternly, "you know that you're not supposed to drink. I'm trying to save you because I love you so much."

He sighed, shook his head and wandered off, leaving the whiskey dripping down the paneled wall. Much later, in New York, his diabetes would have disastrous consequences.

Although the area usually voted Labor, my father, backed by the local Conservative Party, won a seat on the town council, the first Tory ever to represent the area. Typically, he then proceeded to ignore directives from his party and voted for what he called "the best interests of my constituents" Since this usually ran counter to the Conservative policy of freedom to stamp on the undeserving poor when they got uppity, the local Tory Pooh-Bahs were furious. My dad won two terms but lost his third campaign, perhaps because he surrendered to pressure from the right to dump on the poor. If he had won he would have been in line for mayor. One of his stories that I certainly didn't swallow was that at meetings he handed out chewy candy to fellow council members so that when it came time to debate and vote their teeth, caught up in thick toffee, didn't allow them to open their mouths. Still, he told a good, entertaining tale which he clearly enjoyed as much if not more than his audience.

My pretty mother had a kind heart. When we girls were naughty, she would give us some pennies and order us to go to a nearby shop and buy a cane so that she could wallop us. When we came back with the cane, she couldn't bring herself to administer the punishment. Instead, we would get a scolding. What a softie. Later, I opened a closet and found more than twenty canes lying there, unused.

She had an interesting if slightly scandalous history. Her story was that her mother, our grandmother, once had a brief affair with one of the American acting Barrymore's, perhaps the flamboyantly ego-driven John, and as a result produced my mother.

Google tells us that the name of the Barrymore patriarch born in 1849 was Herbert Arthur Chamberlayne Blythe, (what a mouthful). He came from an upper class English family, went to Harrow and Oxford then was destined to become a barrister. However, he fell in love with the stage and, to save his relatives from the shame of having a family member becoming an actor, he changed his name to Maurice Barrymore. He made his way to America and first appeared on Broadway in December 1875. Thus began the legendary, if erratic, careers of the Barrymores.

Apart from the embarrassment of an illegitimate arrival, my mother's birth was a problem because granny already had two other children out of wedlock. Bit of a swinger, granny. The family decided enough was enough and collected sufficient money to buy her a ticket for an Atlantic crossing so that she and her children could move in with relatives living in America, well away from the scene of her anti-social behavior. The chosen British ocean liner was the Lusitania

My mother never boarded the Lusitania because on the ship's voyage early in the second year of World War 1 from New York to the U.K. the vessel was torpedoed by a German U-boat and sunk with the loss of more than a thousand lives. The Germans excused themselves by insisting the liner was carrying not just innocent passengers but munitions and other supplies for the British troops on the Western Front which was probably true. Grandmother and mom stayed in the U.K.

It seems now that this story of the Barrymore connection may well be factual for when my mother died her birth certificate was found and it gave her maiden name, not as we thought Johnson, but as Blythe, the original family name of the Barrymore's. In a small tribute to her, when I later published some books I used the pen name, "Leonora Blythe."

Then there was my Uncle Bob who claimed to be psychic. For instance, he said that during the war he was assigned to General Eisenhower's staff as a camouflage expert. In France one night he dreamed that if their convoy of vehicles (not including Eisenhower's) took a certain route the next day it would be ambushed by the Wehrmacht.

"Oh, get off it," scoffed his colleagues.

"No, mon, I'm telling you, I dreamed the whole scene." After an argument, he was allowed, with a couple of men inclined to believe him, to use a Jeep and take a different route. Of course, the scoffers were ambushed and he was not. Well, it might be true.

David Petreus, the general and CIA chief who fell from grace in a sex scandal, described his father's attitude towards him as "gruff love" which fitted my father pretty well with a bit of bullying tossed in. Our family included our long-suffering but cheery mum, who had hidden literary ambitions, we four girls, a grandmother and aunt, living a few blocks away, our housekeeper/cook, Mrs. Beachy and the cleaner, Mrs. Brown. Father would declare, "I'm hemmed in by females and the dog's a bitch too."

It couldn't have been easy for him. We girls were noisy, competitive, argumentative, inclined to dramatic exits from the turbulence of the dinner table, known as storming off, always out to dominate the others, verbally or physically. As the youngest of the sisters I felt I was victimized but they all probably felt the same. Because in our early years I was the smallest, I was called—and still am—"Titch", a Briticism for small. But nicknames can cut. At school, there was a very bright, engaging and popular girl who was nicknamed "Ant" as in "Antique" because we thought she was a bit old fashioned. . . . But she was cool so we all loved her and used the nickname casually without thought as a sign of our affection for her. In my last years at school she confided to us that every time she heard the word, she mentally flinched. She hated it. We had no idea. We abandoned the horrid word.

At home on the positive side, we occupied a large house, maybe 20 rooms, so there was always somewhere to hide and escape the racket. Father's gruff side was illustrated by his habit of insisting that his darling daughters must be home, say, by 10 p.m. If one of us arrived even a few minutes late, she would find him standing on the doorstep ostentatiously tapping the face of his watch. Get home even later and look out.

He had an odd sense of humor, together with false teeth. While dining out with the family he liked to take out his teeth, put them on the table and, pointing to them, tell the waiter to bring the teeth a glass of water. He thought it was highly amusing. Sensitive us, we squirmed with embarrassment, pretended we'd never seen him before, just happened to be sitting at the same table. But often the waiter would nod and bring the water.

At one point he became enthusiastically involved in the invention/marketing of paper panties for women,—"knickers" in the mother tongue as in, be calm, "Don't get your knickers in a twist." The idea was that hygienically-minded ladies would wear them for a day and then discard them for a fresh pair. The response from women, hygienic or not, was lackluster and he stopped talking about them.

Then there was the ruckus over the telephone in the hall. Father grew more and more exasperated when he went to use it, perhaps for an important discussion of paper panties, only to find one of us in possession. He knew how to deal with that. He contacted the telephone company and had a pay-phone installed. No matter how urgent our need to talk to a boy friend, we had to come up with hard cash. We didn't have much. Problem solved.

Bedeviled by so many daughters, each entitled to a birthday celebration, he ruled that every year we would have one party for all of us which would cover Christmas and our birthdays. For this he would hire the church hall. We each were allowed to invite 10 guests. Before we went away to school, we took ballet lessons and at the party were expected to climb on the stage and demonstrate our expertise. Tres embarrassing.

The question of whether father had ever worked for the British intelligence agency, MI6, arose much later during my time in Manhattan and was never fully resolved, mainly because the tiny possibility that his claim was true hardly seemed worth investigating even if it could have been. "Dear MI6, Sorry to bother you but would you be kind enough to tell me whether my dad, James Fairclough of Ty-Cornell, Allt-yr-ryn Avenue, Newport, Wales, was one of your courageous and devil-may-care agents?"

What is certain is that the trucking firm he ran in Newport went bankrupt and as a result I was pulled out of school in England before I graduated. A problem with school fees. The story was that over a period of many years father's long-trusted accountant had pocketed large amounts of money meant for the tax collector and ended up in a lunatic asylum, one way of escaping the Fairclough wrath.

My education brought to a sudden halt, I decided to take up nursing in London which would remove me from the clamor of the family bedlam and perhaps satisfy a growing hunger for adventure. Did I aim to emulate Florence Nightingale, the lady with the lamp? Not really. London in the 60s was supposed to be swinging and that sounded like my kind of town. I became a trainee at the Royal Masonic Hospital in Hammersmith.

One thing I had learned by the age of 18 was that a robust sense of humor and a refusal to take anything very seriously could give you passage through any crisis, however stark. In short, laugh it off. But I was to learn after six months of training that laughter couldn't conquer every dark situation. I was assigned to the cancer ward, full of terminally-ill patients, because I was, the Matron said, "such a cheerful soul."

The whispers around the hospital corridors were that a Sister, a senior nurse, had committed suicide because of depression caused by dealing day after day, night after night, with dying men and women. And then I walked into a patient's room and found him standing in his hospital gown on the sill at a large open window several floors above the tarmac outside.

"What are you doing?" I screamed. He turned and stared at me blankly. But I knew, oh, I knew just what he was doing and I scuttled over to frantically press the panic button for urgent help. I stood there helplessly, scared to do anything that might precipitate what mustn't happen. We stared at each other. "Please," I whispered, "Oh, please." Then they came rushing in and while I watched they managed to talk him back down into the room so that he could continue to confront his approaching end. He died not long after.

I wasn't so cheery after that. It was one situation where humor, a good laugh, was utterly useless. A month or so later I quit. Cowardice? Perhaps. I just knew that while some brave nurses could survive the bleak atmosphere of pain and death, I couldn't. Having left the hospital, I felt much better. I looked for a more rewarding way of life.

I found the perfect job with a company called Barbour Index, boring name but for me there was nothing boring about it. The firm had been launched by Patrick Barbour, a lanky, hard-driving character still in his 20s, who had invented a much sought-after filing system. He then recruited a squadron of young women, trained them, gave them defined areas to cover across Britain, put them in Mini cars and sent them off to file documents, brochures, advertising leaflets, etc., once a month at the offices of architects and building contractors. My region was Essex, Norfolk and Suffolk, which offered plenty of delightful country to savor. I could be on the road for a month at a time. I suppose the attraction for his customers was that they did not have to hire employees to do the job, which was by no means simple but not too demanding once you had grasped the principle.

This was the 60s when any London girl with legs wore mini-skirts, usually so short they barely covered a lady's bum. Part of Barbour's genius lay in hiring attractively lissome, leggy creatures who brought a welcome touch of glamour when they blew into customers' offices. He certainly didn't object to them wearing tiny skirts. We were called the "Barbour Girls" which of course was before I switched to become a "Nixon Girl."

For me, the big attraction was independence. We were pretty much our own bosses, not stuck all day in offices but driving around our region, free of supervision so long as we did an efficient job. The salary was good. And it was nice to be greeted by appreciative smiles when we and our mini-skirts arrived to handle customers' filing.

Because I was on the road so much, when in London I stayed with my oldest sister, Ann, now married and making a new life in Battersea. One summer evening we were sitting with drinks on the apartment's balcony when an enormous limousine pulled up below us and Ann's husband, Edmund, with the help of the chauffeur, climbed out. He was pretty successful working at a West End art gallery but all the same . . .

When he came upstairs Ann said, "What was that all about?"

"Oh," said Edmund, "some bloke called Mick Jagger was buying stuff at the gallery and he offered me a ride home. A rocker, I believe. Anything to drink?" Hell, couldn't he have invited the rocker up for a drink with us? Edmund, never my favorite person in the world, eventually split with Ann after producing two children and went to Australia to make a name for himself as an art expert. Australia was far away enough to satisfy me.

To jump far ahead, I later learned from a newspaper account that around 1999 Barbour sold his stake in the company, by then presumably using the internet rather than young women, to a French outfit for more than $30 million. Well done, Mr. Barbour.

It was fun but after a couple of years I found the attraction of living in London overcame the appeal of the open road. It might have had something to do with a boy friend in London, too.

Ann, who worked in advertising in central London, kept her eyes and ears open for me and eventually instructed me to go and apply for a position with an executive in the film industry. Oooh, the movies!

CHAPTER TWO

The executive who needed a secretary/assistant and got me, turned out to be one of a kind, or sui generis, as we say in my literate, debonair circle. Privately I thought of him as Mr. Smoothy.

He was a film producer with offices on Wardour Street amid the neon lights, shadowy alleys and dubious half-naked lady loiterers of Soho, then the center of the British movie industry or what there was of it. The tawdry ambiance was lightened by the vibrancy of exotic restaurants, some of them very good, the sound of jazz seeping distantly from clubs and the street chatter of its denizens. But Hollywood was a long way away. The firm was called Associated British Pathe and my new boss was the managing director. He produced documentaries, newsreels, commercials and B-minus movies, anything that needed a camera or two.

Life was hectic with Mr. Smoothy, a fast-talking salesman-type, expensively dressed with a round closely barbered head like a ripe cantaloupe. I was set to work typing scripts, taking dictation, making phone calls, helping entertain and charm visitors, generally making myself useful. If invited, I would even offer a comment on film rushes or commercials. If there was glamour in the film industry, not much penetrated our offices. After a while I thought, "Hello, something's happening here."

Mr. Smoothy had dispatched a film crew and a band of actors to Africa to make some sort of adventure film. The names of the actors escape me although I'm pretty sure they did not include Laurence Olivier or John Gielgud. But now there was something furtive in the air. Mr. Smoothy would make long telephone calls with his door firmly closed. He would argue with the office accountant and then refuse to see him.

My attention was caught when Mr. Smoothy instructed me to type a script for the crew in Africa that was entirely different from the one they had gone out to film. Also, he swore me to secrecy, all in whispers, saying that when I used the print room for the new script and other stuff connected with it I was to make sure nobody else was nearby.

Finally it all got to be too much and he realized that he had to reveal all. He admitted that in truth he was engaged in a spot of deceit. Only the accountant and the musical director knew what was going on. And now me.

He was piggy-backing a second film on the first for his own financial benefit. Out of his own pocket he had paid the crew and actors to make the second movie in Africa after they had completed the first. By using the company's equipment and film stock—with the travel expenses covered by the company—he would have his very own film at an enormous saving to Mr. Smoothy.

While I admired his entrepreneurial initiative, all this made me very uneasy as if I were an accomplice to skullduggery. Rescue however was at hand in the person of Stanley Dudelson, an American film executive. Dudelson was in London contacting Pathe, among other film companies around the world, in search of B-films that could be bought cheaply and sold to American TV, then ravenously hungry for any material that would fill their early morning or late hours of broadcasting. His chief buyer was ABC television, then represented by two little-known executives, Barry Diller and Michael Eisner.

During his time in London, I had been put in charge of arranging the Pathe films for him to review for the firm American International Television, an arm of American International Pictures, celebrated for such epics as Muscle Beach Party, Ghost in the Invisible Bikini and the never to be forgotten How to Stuff a Wild Bikini. We had a pleasant working relationship and before the African movies crisis blew up, he had suggested that I might like to take a job as his secretary in New York. At that time it was chic for American executives to have English secretaries.

Wow! Lanky cowboys, skyscrapers, murderous gangsters, flashing lights on Broadway, film stars, corrupt politicians. Marvelous. A yearning for adventure played a part in my decision to go. I believed that adventure depended on not knowing what was around the corner. I always hoped for something different, even fascinating. I certainly didn't know what awaited me around the American corner but whatever it was, it would certainly be different and perhaps fun, for a little while anyway. For me, growing up in the dreary war years and then the post-war regime of austerity in bankrupt Britain, America shimmered on the horizon like a beautiful irresistible mirage. I was fascinated. America was represented to me by Jimmy Stewart and Gary Cooper, tough but with a tender side. By Ernest Hemingway's audacious, free-swinging heroes. On film, in books, in plays, Americans unlike Brits were willing to show their emotions. I was a little bit in love with the idea of it. Also, I wanted to learn to fly. I wanted the freedom of the skies, the freedom that comes with complete control, with nobody hovering and telling me what to do. The clincher was the thought that flying would be an adventure. Lessons were too expensive for me in the U.K. but I had heard it was manageable in the States. As for romance, a handsome American millionaire wouldn't come amiss either.

And I sensed big trouble looming for Mr Smoothy and perhaps those around him. So I graciously accepted the offer, resigned from Wardour Street and set about applying for a green card at the U.S. embassy in Grosvenor Square. There I learned that it was essential to be able to prove I wouldn't arrive in the States and immediately become an unemployed bimbo lounging around Skid Row while sucking on the government nipple.

A letter from Stanley Dudelson, formally offering me the job, was a big help. Then there was the question of money. I had to have enough to prove I could support myself without government help. However, the officials wouldn't say how much was necessary. Obviously what I needed was every penny I could lay my hands on.

I borrowed from every relative and friend in sight, ending up with about 3,000 pounds, a very healthy sum in those days. After flourishing my bank account documents around Grosvenor Square, I was awarded the essential green card and returned the money to its nervous owners.

CHAPTER THREE

In America, disillusion showed it teeth. At first, I thought I couldn't bear it and would have to go back. I was homesick. Some adventurer you were, Leonora. I longed for the irreverent cockney banter of Soho, for the mountains of mid-Wales where the army's Special Forces play their lethal games and for the lilting Welsh voices. Oh, the shiver up the spine, the tears, as thousands of Welsh rugby fans sang "Land of my Fathers" while we beat the cocky England team at Cardiff Arms Park. America was horrible. A rainy Sunday in Manchester would be better than this. Americans struck me as childishly boastful, militaristic, proud of their clinically crazy gun culture, grasping, rude and arrogant yet oddly prudish—don't call it the lavatory, call it the toilet or the bathroom. And they ate far too much. When dining out, I would be confronted with a plate of food as big as the state of Rhode Island and immediately lose my appetite.

Crime? Forgedaboutdit. While others dubbed it the Land of Opportunity, to me it was the Land of Grabit and Run.

Violent culture clash.

Mini skirts had not arrived in New York but they were the only skirts in my wardrobe so I wore them without a thought. On my way to work I walked past a building site and one day a husky young hard hat standing with his laughing mates tossed a 20 dollar bill at my feet.

I didn't know what the implication was but I suspected it was not good. I bent, maneuvering to keep my skirt decent, picked up the bill, gave him the lethal Fairclough glare and handed it back to him. He took it silently and, I hope, was suitably shamed.

In Times Square another time, I looked right instead of left and was hit by a cab. It was my fault and all I got was torn stockings and a bruise or two. But suddenly a man rushed to my side and said he was a lawyer. He thrust a card at me. "Give me a call," he said.

"What for?" I asked although I suspected I knew. "It was my fault and no harm's done"

"There might be something in it for you. You never know. Call me." He wasn't an ambulance chaser; he was a taxi chaser. Throwing his card away, I thought what sort of country was this where lawyers prowled the streets like hungry wolves?

Aggressive commercialism was everywhere. I was bewildered. Turn on the radio and one advertisement followed another with pitchmen shouting at me. The same on TV. Everybody in New York seemed to be in a frantic race to make money. They walked fast—pausing only to spit gobs expertly on the sidewalk—talked fast, ate fast, drove fast, none of the quiet, slow delights of good food, good music, good books, good conversation, the simple pleasures of being alive, no time for anything but pursuit of the dollar.

I remembered an old story that had some truth to it. It went like this: A British working man sees a large, chauffeured limousine cruising by, a plutocrat smoking a cigar in the back. The Brit stares resentfully, then picks up a brick and hurls it at the limo. An American blue collar worker sees the same limo and its passenger. He says, "That's great. One day I'll sit in a limo like that, smoking a cigar." The American dream. Me? I'd look at the limo and think, "If I had that sort of money I'd buy a James Bond-engineered Aston Martin, much more fun." The Leonora dream.

What annoyed me was that so many Americans were comfortably ignorant about the world beyond their borders. They knew they were the greatest people in the world living in the greatest city in the greatest country in the world. Anything outside America was of no importance or interest. They knew they alone had won the war, They knew nothing and cared nothing about Canadians, Australians, Indians, Chinese, New Zealanders, British, Poles, Soviets (20 million dead) who had been struggling for years before the U.S. was dragged in. They thought they had gallantly decided to take on Hitler after Pearl Harbor. They didn't seem to know that Hitler had foolishly decided to declare war on them. They were so incurious that they didn't know the origin of the term, "Empire State." I wanted to fill in that gap in my knowledge so I called a state historian in Albany. He said that George Washington, after a visit to New York State, was so impressed with its potential that he declared it could be the seat of empire, an odd remark for somebody exiting the British Empire.

"We're Number One!" New Yorkers blustered. If you're really number one, old sport, you wouldn't need to shout it because it would be self-evident. A dash of humility would have been lovely.

Racists? There was racism in Britain but nothing approaching that in America. In the South where they talked funny; black Americans whose families often had been in the States decades longer than many of the nitwits oppressing them were barred on ridiculous grounds from voting—"What's the last word of the Sixth Amendment?" That was when white Southerners weren't busy lynching blacks and blowing up their churches with children inside. Down there, discrimination was so pervasive that Congress decided in the 60s that it would be ever so nice if black citizens could vote just like white citizens and passed a law to that effect. As for American Indians, who had owned the country until Europeans decided they wanted it, they were not allowed to be citizens until 1924. In Britain, at least, they didn't proudly sing about "the land of the free and the home of the brave."

When much later I learned more about the hallowed Constitution and innocently suggested to Americans that it was stuck in the mud of history, inflexible and outdated—guns for everybody, yeah! How about an AK-47?—the atmosphere turned sour. In contrast, Britain had no written constitution. Instead the country relied on a collection of laws, precedents and traditions vague enough that they could be revised with relative ease in the light of modern events and needs. Sloppy maybe, compared with a written constitution, but it worked because it was not a rigid set of rules. And there was no bench of nine unelected men and women who could block the will of the people on the basis of a document written 230 years ago by founders, some of them slave-holders, who had no concept of life today.

Yeah, they said, but what about Britain's monarchy, the country ruled by an unelected queen? She has little to do with it, I explained. She does not rule; she reigns. Now that the House of Lords has been neutered, power rests almost entirely with the House of Commons where members are elected directly by the people. If the government fails spectacularly it can be turned out swiftly with a vote of no confidence in Parliament and replaced in a matter of weeks. A more efficient democracy? I think so but I learned not to innocently suggest any such thing.

I had to admit that the British national anthem, "God Save Our Queen/King." was pretty silly. Save them from what? Also, there were the British libel laws, a disgrace and a shocking impediment to free speech. Wealthy people from around the world who could afford expensive lawyers went shopping to the London law courts where they knew they would find a legal system tilted in their favor if they came under literary or verbal assault, even if the defendant spoke or wrote nothing but the truth. Essentially it was part of the class system. The bewigged barristers might as well have put up a sign outside the Royal Courts of Justice: "If you are wealthy and upper class and aggrieved by written facts, we can sooth your pain by beggaring your opponent." Score an important point for the U.S. constitution and its first amendment.

There was of course the problem of the weather in the U.K. But the Brits could hardly be blamed for that.

Then there was the health issue, or lack of it. How could a country call itself civilized in the last half of the 20th century when it failed to look after its people with some sort of universal health service? I know, I know. Many Americans had been asking the same question for years. Even my hero, Richard Nixon, had proposed universal health care with employers mandated to pay for health insurance for their workers. It went nowhere.

Opponents dismissed such ideas with the nightmarish word, Socialism, although not many people knew what it meant. Another version of Communism, they were told, and the politicians ran like rabbits.

Worse still, Americans didn't know how to make chocolates. Their version was ghastly, uneatable. Oh, stop whining, Leonora, even if the Brits have made grumbling an art form. You're a cheerful soul, remember.

To comfort myself in my misery I would call the British airline, BOAC, and ask if they had a seat that night on a London flight. If the answer was yes, I wouldn't buy a ticket but I hugged the thought that I could have and in less than 12 hours be back in London. I gave that up when they began to recognize my voice and politely complained that I never actually bought a ticket.

I wasn't the only Fairclough in the States. Bridget, my second oldest sister, was living in Oklahoma with her husband, Richard, who was doing some sort of time and motion study for the state government. Bridget, a nurse in England, was working at the local hospital. She invited me to join them for Thanksgiving and so I flew down. We went around to some neighbors to celebrate the big day. What a strange bunch. Every room in the house seemed to have a TV set tuned to a football game and the male guests just sat there staring at the screen uttering the occasional cry of triumph or, more often, a howl of anguish that belonged in a torture chamber. The women were confined to the kitchen. It was nice to see Bridget but I've never been back to Oklahoma.

Of course it wasn't all revolting. I loved the sly wit of senatorial poet and presidential candidate Gene McCarthy. When an opponent, George Romney, complained that he had been brainwashed by the U.S. generals in Viet Nam, McCarthy said that a "light rinse" would have done the job. Also, "Being in politics is like being a football coach. You have to be smart enough to understand the game and dumb enough to think it's important."

Before Watergate, politics compared with the moneyed horrors of today were relatively gentlemanly or should I say lady-like. Cash was not in complete control.

In fairness, I had to admit that while there was a class system in America, it was not as deadly and perverse as that back home. See the beloved Eve Waugh. Also see P.G. Wodehouse who wrote benignly about Hooray Henrys who, after getting drunk, would run around London bravely knocking off the helmets of constables. That was all right because they were of the upper class and the policemen were not. Let a Covent Garden porter try it, not that he ever would, and he would receive much rougher treatment. Professor Higgins was right. An Englishman or woman only had to speak one sentence and he/she were slotted into their class, their place in life. Why the Welsh, Scots and Irish escaped the system and were not similarly classified I did not know.

I was making some friends, although mostly ex-pats. One of them was Carol, a beautiful British stewardess with TWA, who had talked to Dudelson on one of his flights back to America. He told her about my approaching arrival and said that perhaps I might like to share her penthouse apartment with her and two other stewardesses, both with Pan Am, which is what happened. Actually, penthouse was a bit of a misnomer. The apartment was merely the top one of a four or five storey building. Carol was to play a significant role in my future. Unfortunately we had to vacate the apartment shortly after I had moved in because the landlord needed it for his good and extremely close friend, the gorgeous Hollywood star, Tab Hunter.

Carol introduced me to one of her courtiers, who shook my hand and said, "Brooks Keller, Secret Service, at your service." He then plucked a card from his pocket and handed it to me. It read, "Brooks Keller, Secret Service." Seeing my raised eyebrows he explained that he was an agent of the Secret Service dedicated, among other things, to the protection of the President and his family. But that wasn't why my eyebrows elevated. It struck me as extremely odd that a member of the Secret Service was running around announcing to everybody who he was. Surely that was supposed to be a secret. Keller then invited me to accompany him to the theater on a mission. With Carol away flying, he needed me to make a couple. He explained that he was in New York to protect the President's daughter, Lynda Johnson, who with her brand new husband, Charles Robb, was going to the theater the following night. To be less noticeable than sitting on his own, he needed a lady, me, to give him cover. I agreed to help. We sat behind LBJ's daughter to make sure that nobody tried to shoot her or blow her up. I didn't see all of the performance because I was so busy scanning the audience for homicidal maniacs or terrorists. I also watched for any overly-aggressive autograph hunters The audience looked respectable enough but, of course, a murderous fiend would make sure he looked perfectly normal to disguise his intent. In fact, nothing untoward happened and Brooks Keller was a perfect gentleman, just as you would expect of a government worker. I didn't hope for a reward for taking part in an undercover operation, a medal or anything like that. I had just done my duty, my little bit, to keep the republic on an even course. You're welcome.

One day, Dudelson took me for lunch at Sardi's, the favorite haunt of show business folk. Coming out, we encountered a little band of autograph hunters. One of the fans approached me and asked for an autograph. God knows who she thought I was but, what the hell, I signed her little book with elan. With my writing, she wouldn't be able to decipher the signature anyway. What fun and it seemed to make her happy.

Slowly I realized I had been making a huge mistake that had controlled my view of this new country. Because of the almost common language, I hadn't thought of the States as a foreign land when in fact it was as foreign as, say, Paraguay or Hungary. For goodness sake, lighten up, Leonora. Better to look at Americans as alien curiosities. Better to have a good laugh at the weird attitudes. If I were surrounded by Paraguayans or Hungarians I would have accepted the crazy way they ran their countries, probably thinking, How sweet, how exotic, how different. I had wanted adventure, I told myself, and like it or not here I was in the middle of one. After that I felt more comfortable but it was still a strange land with strange ideas of its superiority to other countries.

Then, a few months after my arrival in New York, I woke up one morning to see summer sunshine outside the windows, the air fresh, fragrant, and I astonished myself by thinking, "I quite like it here after all. I think I'll stay." That didn't mean I would stay for ever. A year or two, perhaps, and then back to good old London.

I enjoyed the people I worked with, being a Nixon girl had been a laugh and where else would I be stopped for an autograph or go undercover for the White House? I was even picking up the lingo. And I was getting used to the Manhattan light infantry quick-march tempo.

By then, I had discovered that for 20 dollars a lesson I could learn to fly at Teterborough, a little airport in New Jersey, across the Hudson from Manhattan. That probably had something to do with my change of attitude. During my first lesson, Frank, the instructor and a nice man, took me up for a little flight around the region. It was a revelation. Down below I could see Manhattan, the towers, now tiny, looking like fingers pointing to the future and, off to the west, I could see fading into the horizon the limitless hills and fields and forests of this vast country.

Frank, sitting alongside me in the Cessna 150, let me take the dual controls for a few minutes while keeping his hands lightly on his flight stick in case I did something silly. I was overwhelmed with a feeling of freedom, in charge, floating high above the ordinary workaday world. I was hooked.

Some weeks later, mother and father came over to see what I was up to. Mom stayed on the ground but dad eagerly accepted an offer to go aloft. Frank took us up, cruising down the Hudson alongside the skyscrapers, around the Battery and up the East River. Dad was goggle-eyed. He loved every minute. We were close enough to see people in their offices, doing their dreary jobs, some staring out at us. Whoopee. When we landed back at Teterborough, however, officials with grim expressions were waiting. They accused us of flying too close to the towers of Manhattan, there had been complaints and, "Dammit, don't you dare do it again." But that was the end of it. Try it today after 9/11 and you'd probably be shot down by NYPD ground-to-air missiles.

Worse, much worse, was to come. On a Saturday some weeks later I went out to Teterborough to take a written test for my license. Afterwards I saw Frank, who was about to take a couple of more advanced students down to Red Bank, New Jersey, in a four-seater Cessna 172 to do some touch-and-go landings in which your wheels touch down and then instead of stopping you immediately take off again. He invited me to take the fourth seat and have a free joy ride. Sure. I settled into the passenger seat behind the pilot's position and off we went. The touch-and-goes were accomplished succesfully and we took off, heading back to home base. I was still sitting behind the pilot, this time a student named Zack. That was when it happened.

Not long after take-off, at about 1,000 feet, the engine cut out. One minute it was burbling along nicely, the next it coughed, fell silent, just died. Zack froze. My reaction was noisier, "Shit!" Adventures were fun but, hell, mine wasn't supposed to include this. I thought this was the end. I was gripping the armrest so hard my hands hurt.

Immediately Frank said, "I've got it" and took over the controls although all he could control was where we would come down. As we sank lower and lower, he tried and failed to restart the engine. No response. For me, time was whipping by at warp speed. Suddenly we were frighteningly close to the ground. Frank looked desperately for somewhere to land. Ahead was a housing complex, to the right was a forest. To the left was a big parking lot which normally on a Saturday like this would be empty. Frank could have gotten us down there, no problem. But it belonged to a telephone company which had just settled a strike. As a result the lot was full of the cars of workers who were getting back up to speed. It was the only possibility.

Frank was brilliant. "Check your seat belts. Hold tight," he said, as if I could hold any tighter. He was so cool. His hands steady on the controls, staring fixedly ahead, he brought the plane, silent but for the rush of the wind, gliding down to the edge of the parking lot. Nobody spoke. The plane began to bounce off the top of the cars while we were jerked around like dice in a cup. We could hear the undercarriage crunching on the car roofs. The first car later turned out to be a vintage model owned by the local police chief. We bounced off the next and then the next, six or seven in all. We had slowed but were still traveling with enough force that when we came off the last car we smashed in a riot of noise into a barrier of trees where, thank God, the Cessna finally stopped.

Thanks not to God but to Frank, we were down. No veteran airline pilot, no-hot-shot top gun, could have done a more skillful job. Frank should have been awarded some sort of medal. On the other hand, he didn't need a medal. He knew that he had saved four lives, including his own, and that probably was enough for him. As a bit of a skeptic, I suspected that most medals went to the wrong people anyway. In that line of thinking, I hate it when civilians say to someone in the military, "Thank you for your service." It makes me cringe. It costs nothing and that's what it's worth. It's as easy and meaningless as a bumper sticker saying, "We support our troops."

Three of us were lucky. One wasn't. A tree branch had pierced the front of the plane and pinned Zack in his seat which rocketed back and gashed my right leg. Zack, who had just canceled his health insurance, was seriously injured, perhaps paralyzed. My leg was bleeding but it was minor compared with Zack's injuries. The instructor, Frank, who had saved our lives, suffered a broken, bloody nose. Bobby, the fourth victim who had medical insurance, barely got a scratch. We were all shaken up but so thankful that we had survived.

Rescuers came running. Zack, unconscious, was extricated with difficulty from his seat which allowed me to slide out of the plane. Siren blaring, an ambulance arrived and took us all to a hospital to be examined and patched up. Three of us left to find the plane that Teterborough had sent to pick us up. Zack stayed.

I don't know how the telephone workers felt when they saw their smashed cars but it was a subdued trio that arrived back at our home airport. For me, some of the blithe confidence I had felt in the air had leaked. Probably it was good that we flew back to Teterborough, like getting back in the saddle immediately after being thrown from a naughty horse. I still wanted to fly but after the crash I looked at Cessnas with some suspicion. I was to have good reason.

Later, we returned to the parking lot to survey the wreckage of the plane and somebody took a photograph of us which I still have. My body language in the picture conveyed severe disapproval. We visited Zack in the hospital and there was talk of suing Cessna for their plane's failure in the hope he could to raise enough money to cover his medical and rehab expenses. I don't know if anything came of it.

Towards the end of my training I was sent up to complete a 100-mile solo flight, no instructor alongside me. The weather was fine and I was enjoying myself high above the forests of Pennsylvania when the instruments on the panel in front of me went haywire. They weren't showing what they should. If I turned right they didn't show a right turn. The same with any maneuver I made. Hell, with no instruments to guide me, I was lost over Pennsylvania, no idea where I was or what I should do. This time there was no experienced pilot like Frank to take over.

It turned out all right. I was in radio contact with Teterborough which had me on their radar screens. "Number one: Don't panic," they ordered. Easy for them to say. "Number two: Do exactly as I direct you." They then talked me down to a Pennsylvania airstrip where I was later picked up by a plane from Teterborough. Thank you, Mr. Radar. No thanks to you, Mr. Cessna.

At Teterborough, I think they were getting quite used to sending a plane to pick me up from distant airfields. One more and I could imagine somebody saying to a pilot, "It's HER again. Off you go."

I noted that, during my many hours of training, I never saw another woman studying to become a pilot. Maybe there was a flock of them that I never saw or maybe American women were too busy fighting discrimination to have adventures in the air.

My training completed, I was scheduled to make a final visit to Teterborough before receiving my pilot's license. I was to go up with an examiner and display my skills at flying to another airfield, emergency landing, touch-and-go, all the basic knowledge which would allow me to call myself a pilot.

The first time I called in to check on the weather they said, "Forget it today. It's socked in. Try again." Same thing the second day I called. The third time, it was the same. Lousy weather, clouds too low. A pity but I was beginning to get a message. Maybe I wasn't meant to win my license. I never called again and I never got my license.

Anyway, another interest had intervened.

CHAPTER FOUR

One day, Carol invited me to join her that evening for cocktails with a couple of her followers in the Oak Bar at the Plaza. It sounded sophisticated, cool, so I dropped by on my way to a lesson at Teterborough. Two Brits were sitting there gazing devotedly at Carol but there was no million dollar aura around either of them.

One, a character with the classic lean and hungry look, was introduced as Tony and he stood up to shake hands. Well-trained, I thought. With Teterborough ahead, I couldn't drink but I sat down and chatted for a few moments. It seemed that Tony, once a Royal Marine, had been knocking around America in a TR3 sports car, managing to drive through Arizona blissfully unaware that he had sailed right past the Grand Canyon until he looked at a map the next day, quite an achievement. He defended himself by saying that it was just a big hole in the ground. He ended up as a reporter with the Daily News which was on 42nd St. across Second Avenue from my apartment. He lived 10 blocks north. He said he had sworn an oath he would never live in a place where he couldn't walk to work in 20 minutes and pack all his belongings in one large suitcase and leave in another 20 minutes. Hah! That was an oath that would be well and truly shattered. After exchanging pleasantries I went on my way.

A few days later, this Tony called me with an odd request. He wanted to know if I had a piece of medium-size luggage he could borrow. The News was dispatching him to Florida on a roving assignment and he didn't have the appropriate hold-all for his fresh shirts and undies. His one suit-case was too big. Uh, oh, I thought, another Brit on the con. In New York, visiting Brits were notorious for trying to take advantage of the yokel locals. "Oh! My dear fellow. It's just a loan for a few days. Would I cheat you? I went to Eton and Oxford, don't you know." Still, I noted that his sense of humor ran on the same absurd track as mine but fretted that was part of a con.

I decided to take a chance on him. He came round, inspected my luggage and announced that one piece would be perfect. Off he went with it while I wondered if that would be the last I would see of Tony and my suitcase. Suspicious me. A couple of weeks later he and the borrowed luggage reappeared. Much obliged, he said, and would I let him take me for dinner as a thank-you? We went to Annette's Petit Veau on Second Avenue, long gone now, where they did a great sole amandine. In the French style, Annette sat with her cash register by the door so that she could monitor restaurant activities and make sure that no customer could escape without paying. Over dinner, Tony told me he belonged to the family that had produced the 17th century Oxford don, Robert Burton, who despised women and bathing and published the tome, The Anatomy of Melancholy. Fascinating, up to a point. It occurred to me that the ancient Burton's phobia about bathing would make women despise him as well. Tony also told me he admired my teeth, which was funny, because they were already a mess, preparing to get worse. I fluttered my eyelashes prettily at him. That had the desired effect. Annette's was to become our favorite spot. That was the start of a relationship that was to last for more than 40-years and continues today.

While I was learning to fly I was also learning that you can have a surfeit of Japanese, Spanish, German, films with sub-titles. Working for Dudelson, one of my tasks was to sit and watch foreign movies to see if they could be packaged for sale to American TV. Much later Dudelson was to produce the Nightmare on Elm Street movies. For me, sitting watching these second or third rate films hour after hour in a screening room became a minor nightmare on Broadway. Even today I can't bear to watch films with sub-titles. I jumped ship.

I went to work for Warner Brothers which, financially sick, was about to become part of Steve Ross's surging entertainment and communication empire. It began with a funeral parlor and ended up as a multi-million dollar conglomerate sprawled from coast to coast. My new boss was film producer Fred Weintraub, a street-wise, rangy bloke from the Bronx with a beard and a pony-tail, who wore jeans and an open neck shirt, never a suit and tie. He was awarded the title of Vice President of Creative Services but the corporate style was out, the hipster long-hairs were in—up to a point—some suits and number-crunchers were still to be found. Also in, at last, were mini skirts.

This was a time when you couldn't walk through Times Square without sniffing the pungent whiff of substances that were not tobacco. Sometimes that whiff could be caught in the corridors of Warner's, obviously from a visitor because no staff members would ever break the law. Even so, there were stories that bags of pot could be found in filing cabinets under the letters MJ for Mary Jane, probably a joke that became a rumor. Pot never appealed to me; the only time I tried a smoke it left me feeling ill.

Fred Weintraub had founded the Bitter End, the club in Greenwich Village where musicians like Bob Dylan, Joni Mitchell, the Mothers of Invention and comedians such as Bill Cosby and Woody Allen among scores of other budding stars made their break-throughs. Now he was at the leading edge of the new wave of movie-makers that was taking over, remaking Warners with more emphasis on filming on the east coast. Hollywood East. He was a good boss, laid back, funny, but serious about movies and open to new ideas. He was always ready to fight to the quitting point for films that he believed in.

At the end of the 1960s, they were making "Klute", a silly, pretentious film set in New York with a nonsensical plot that nonetheless won Jane Fonda an Oscar for her role as a prostitute. Fred was heading out for a lunch appointment when he stopped by my desk and said, "There's a woman coming in to see me. Look after her for me if I'm not back. She's a call girl who's going to advise Fonda on how they operate, their psychology, their psyches, their motivation, all that stuff." Wasn't it Hitchcock who said, "It's only a moo-vie."?

When the receptionist reported that Fred's visitor was here, I went out to escort her in because I wanted to take a good look at the naughty lady. I stared at her and gasped, "Alice?" I knew her.

"Leonora!" she cried. I've always been a hugger and I rushed to embrace her. I had gone to the local school with her in my home town, Newport, before I had been sent away to school and during holidays we occasionally had run into each other shopping or strolling around the town center.

Back in my office I said, "What on earth . . . ?"

"I'm here to give technical advice to Jane Fonda," she said uncomfortably. She still had her Welsh accent.

"Oh, lovely," I said. "Mr. Weintraub will be back soon."

She was a pleasant-featured blonde, smartly dressed in high heels, with a marked Welsh accent who, would not have looked out of place at La Cirque or a gala at the Metropolitan Museum. She could have been a wealthy stockbroker's wife come into town from Scarsdale to do some shopping. Alice certainly didn't look like a call girl to me but then I didn't know what a call girl was supposed to look like. She said she had a little boy being looked after back in Swansea, Wales, by her parents but not much more because Fred came back from lunch and whisked her away into his office.

"Make sure they give you a credit, technical adviser, on the film," I called after her. She smiled and that was the last I saw of her. But on the next St. David's Day (patron saint of Wales) she sent me a bouquet of daffodils (the Welsh national flower) I wrote a note of thanks. A year later I got more daffodils but that was the last I heard of her. She was a nice woman. When "Klute" was finished and I watched it in the screening room I'm sure she got that credit but when, years later, I ran the DVD of the movie I couldn't spot her name on the credits. Maybe I imagined it.

Working for Fred, you had to be ready for anything, from steering Robert Redford to the screening room a floor below past excited office workers who wanted to elbow their way into his exalted presence, to taking Fred's pet, a big black dog, for a relieving walk up and down midtown Fifth Avenue. Musicians and Hollywood stars floated in and out. I was Fred's gatekeeper/assistant/secretary/gofer but it was fun, the main thing.

Fred, who had never operated in the corporate world before, never produced a film and never engaged in office warfare, nonetheless had clout. His office included a bathroom and was lavishly decorated with furniture from the set of the film, "My Fair Lady" which he had found in storage in Hollywood and had shipped to New York. Some of it would end up in my hands.

I gathered that his rival, John Calley in Hollywood, who was head of production, resented Fred's sudden rise from nowhere but top dog of all was Ted Ashley, a former talent agent, an old friend of Fred's and Ashley was in New York. Fred had a most powerful ally.

For me, it seemed there was hardly ever a dull moment in Manhattan. One morning, I was standing at the corner of 51st St. and First Avenue trying to cross First when a smartly dressed woman came rushing up behind me just as the traffic lights turned against us. She didn't stop. She went running across First as the traffic revved up and accelerated forward. Silly woman, obviously not a real New Yorker unless she wanted to commit suicide. A cab, its brakes screeching, hit her and she landed on the hood before sliding to the ground. Traffic slowed and then halted. I went to help her and found her clothes were sadly awry but she didn't seem badly hurt. Where are the police when you need them? In a minor miracle, a cop was immediately on the scene and he took over. The cab driver was distraught. "I had the light," he said. "She came out of nowhere."

"I know," I said. "It was her fault." I felt sorry for him so I scribbled down my name and phone number at Warner's. "Give me a call if you need a witness," I said. I also gave my name and number to the cop before taking advantage of the halted traffic to cross First and pick up my dry cleaning. I thought that was the end of it.

But several months later, big boss Ted Ashley called me into his office. What had I done now?

"Sit down, Leonora," he said. Was he going to fire me, ask me out to dinner?

"A little time ago," he said, "I believe you witnessed an accident on First Avenue."

"Yes, I did. A crazy woman ran into the traffic against the lights."

"Well, that crazy woman is a friend of mine." He said she was the wife of the boss of Columbia Pictures which had a joint distribution deal with Warner's. The light began to dawn.

"I believe you told the police that she was at fault," he said.

"That's right. The traffic coming up First had been given the green light and she tried to run across. She was asking for it."

"You're quite sure that's the way it was, that she was in the wrong?"

"Quite sure."

"No doubts?"

"No doubts." I was disappointing the man who held my future in his hands. How noble of me to cling to the truth

He seemed about to say something more but then he shrugged and said, "Okay, Leonora. Thanks for dropping by."

What was that all about? I remembered the similar incident in Times Square when I collided with a taxi and I remembered the lawyer who wanted to pursue the matter even if it was my fault. All I could think now was that the woman wanted to sue the cab driver, the cab company, the city, the state, the Department of Transportation in D.C., the manufacturer of the traffic light and I was a definite hindrance to any legal action. In fairness to Ted Ashley, I can report I heard no more and I never was penalized for being such a nuisance.

In spite of his splashy acquisitions, Steve Ross still ran the funeral parlors which had launched his extraordinary career. A meeting was held to discuss how to increase revenues in the funeral business; competition was fierce, said a Suit, funereal black of course, and there were only so many corpses to go around. At one point, I chirruped, "What about opening offices in Viet Nam? Lot of potential there." It didn't go down well.

I didn't care. Top of my agenda was marriage and where we were going to have the wedding. Tony and I meshed. Stuffy formal weddings, we thought, were almost barbaric, too often with tensions between families, bawdy jokes, awkward speeches, too much food and drink, even brawls, all the costly ballyhoo of the wedding industry and after the few hours were over bank accounts depleted of cash that could have been better spent on the future of the bride and groom. The celebrations were not so much for the often-embarrassed couple but more for the families and guests.

City Hall? Too bleak and bureaucratic. Church? Neither of us was in the least religious. We thought religion was a joke, although, as it would turn out, the joke was on us. The fountain in Central Park? Muggers.

"What about St. Thomas in the U.S. Virgin Islands" Tony said. He had friends down there. I loved the idea. What an adventure.

"But if we're going down to the Caribbean," I said, "why not go a bit further and do the deed on the British Virgin Islands?" Obviously, I still felt the need of a connection with home. Follow the flag. Tony was agreeable. We wrote to officials in Road Town, the capital of Tortola, and discovered we would have to be able to prove at least a two week residence. The response, tinged with disapproval of the whole idea, said that a "marriage officer" would have to be found if the wedding was to be officially recognized.

"Fine," said Tony. "We'll turn the traditional sequence on its head and have a two week honeymoon before getting married." It was a bit like having the roast beef before the soup but, hell, it all went down the same way. Carol, responsible for the whole thing, God bless her, promised to fly down. How unfortunate that no far-away relatives, as much as we loved them, would be able to attend. Down we went, heading straight for the government offices in Road Town to establish the start of our two week residence.

Tony's friend, Ray Miles, a British photographer, had a wedding present awaiting us. He offered us the use of a beautiful ketch, the Mistress, complete with crew, to take us and any guests from St. Thomas to the rocky little island of Virgin Gorda where the wedding was to be held. He had made a deal with the young Canadian skipper—call him Cap'n Jack because he was as incorrigible as Jack Sparrow—to take pictures for a brochure and instead of payment we would have the use of the Mistress for a couple of days before the owners arrived to take over. Cap'n Jack would have a fellow sailor, Phil, as his first mate. Also, with his wife and kids, generous Ray would sail with us to take pictures. Brilliant.

We spent two weeks having fun in the sun. During that time we picked up rumors that the marriage officer on Virgin Gorda was a whisky priest a la Graham Greene. So it seemed appropriate that we should arrange to meet him at the bar of the Lord Nelson Inn on Virgin Gorda for discussions of the approaching ceremony. The Lord Nelson, a haunt of locals rather than tourists, included a restaurant/bar, a palm-thatched area, open to the soft ocean breezes and was notable for the peacocks strutting about outside. When the vicar appeared, we found that we had been misled. He wouldn't take a drink. It seemed he wasn't the regular pastor but an American substitute from another island.

He was enthusiastic about the wedding. It seemed they hardly ever had them on Virgin Gorda. "We've had an idea," we said. "We'd like to have the ceremony right here at the Lord Nelson. The rustling of the palm leaves is all the music we need."

"Well . . . I don't really like to do weddings in bars," he said delicately. "Why not go up the road to the church? There's really nowhere else."

We weren't in favor of a religious backdrop but so long as it would be a civil ceremony, okay. We set the date and the time.

On the day before the wedding, we set sail under fair skies with Carol, the Miles family and a pleasant bloke, Paul, we had met during our honeymoon who said he would love to join us. He could be an usher even if there was nobody to usher.

After anchoring overnight at Peter Island, we landed the next morning at Road Town on Tortola to pick up our license. Now there was a problem. In fact, disaster. The official Brit said we had been in residence only for 13 days so we couldn't get married until the following day.

"But this is the 14th day even if it isn't yet ended."

"Doesn't matter. It has to be the full 14 days."

"But everything is arranged, the church, the wedding dinner at the Lord Nelson."

"Doesn't matter. Rules are rules."

"Our boat has to be back in St. Thomas by tomorrow morning."

"Rules are rules." God, he was stuffy.

"Surely you can overlook a little rule in the cause of romance, our futures."

"If we do it for you, we'd have to do it for everybody." What, he was conjuring up a vision of thousands of couples pouring into the British Virgins to get married in 13 days? He didn't think it was funny.

There was only one thing for it. I started to cry. The tears ran down my cheeks in rivulets as if from a leaky bowser. He backed away in dismay.

"See what you've done," Tony said sternly.

"Now, look here," he stuttered. More tears. They broke through his colonial crust or perhaps he just wanted to get rid of us and go to lunch. Whatever, he sighed heavily and handed over the papers we needed, breaking the rules and doubtless giving his conscience a lifetime's unease. Amazing how quickly my tears stopped. I noticed that he didn't wish us a long and happy marriage.

We searched Road Town for a wedding bouquet but could only find some sad plastic flowers. They would have to do. We hustled back to the Mistress, raised sail and scudded off to the dock at Virgin Gorda where we had lunch of sandwiches, fruit and champagne, with dunks in the ocean to cool off. A rickety Jeep carried us over rough roads, washed out in a recent series of storms, to the simple, white-washed little church that commanded a magnificent view of the islands. We had a grand total of seven guests if you included the babe in arms belonging to Ray and his wife.

The clergyman was waiting in full regalia, which seemed a bit odd for a civil ceremony. It got odder. As the proceedings proceeded, it became clear—"Let us pray"—that this was a religious ceremony.

Tony and I, happy heathens both, exchanged glances, shrugged and let him go ahead. God had won. The busiest person in attendance was Ray who not only acted as best man but also dodged around frantically taking pictures. I was distracted by itches on my legs from sand flies on the beach. One of the wedding snaps showed me standing on one leg in front of the vicar, using the other to scratch the bites.

When our little group walked out into the sunshine, we found the school next door had just let out and the children, all in smart uniforms, were lined up behind the wire fence to stare at us. I gave a couple of them a hug while Tony stalked along with his hands clasped behind his back like Prince Philip, saying every so often, "Thank you so much for coming," "Thank you for coming." They had no rice, though, to throw at us.

Back aboard the Mistress we triumphantly hoisted a "Just Married" banner. The Lord Nelson was ready for our wedding dinner. So, it turned out, was everybody else on Virgin Gorda. Because of the storms and washed out roads this was the first time that the locals had been able to gather and they were all waiting for us, determined to have a good time. When the wedding party walked into the palm-fringed restaurant/bar, mine host waved a piece of paper at us. My father had sent a handsome check which helped no end in covering the cost of the noisy frolics.

That rambunctious evening I don't remember very well except that. Tony gave a five-word speech, "Thank you all for coming." Who needed rambling speeches? That said it all. In the midst of it, Cap'n Jack came over to me and said, "Awfully sorry, but we're really going to have to leave. Got to have the boat back in St. Thomas first thing tomorrow." But then he vanished.

We later learned that he had fallen under the spell of a young lady and disappeared upstairs with her for an extended period. When he reappeared it was after midnight and we started back to the Mistress, anchored off the beach, swearing and giggling in the dark on the path down to the water. As Cap'n Jack reached for the Boston whaler that was to take us out to our ship he dropped a 50 dollar bill into the briny. "Forget it," we shouted. But he insisted on stripping and diving and, remarkably, came up with the money.

A brisk wind was blowing us toward St. Thomas. We collapsed on deck, bewitched by the phosphorescence in the wake. No time for an overnight on Peter Island. We made it back to Charlotte Amalie just in time. As we walked along the dock we passed the owners, just arrived to go aboard Mistress

We heard later that Phil, who became harbor-master on St. Thomas, lost some toes when his boat banged into the side of one of the cruise liners that visited Charlotte Amallie. Sadly, we also learned that the Mistress was eventually lost at sea.

Back in New York, we unpacked at our 51st St. apartment and I went out to pick up some supplies. When I came back, Tony was packing again.

"What on earth are you doing?"

"They want me on the West Coast."

"Who does? What for?

It was their lordships at the Daily News. Over the years, dinner parties, New Years Eve parties, Thanksgivings would be scrapped at the whim of the editors. In this case, it was a mass murderer called Charlie Manson who attracted their attention and Tony was dispatched to satisfy their curiosity.

CHAPTER FIVE

When Tony eventually returned we went to a party thrown by Ian Brodie, a hack with the London Daily Telegraph. We were introduced to a Dutch girl working at the United Nations. Her name was Xaviera de Vries.

"Be nice to her," Brodie said privately. "She's just been left standing at the altar by her boy friend. She's in a terrible state." We did our best. She was a green-eyed blonde of buxom stature. Her English was good although her accent was quite pronounced.

"You're a reporter for a New York paper?" she said to Tony. "I wonder if you can help me." I was not overly pleased at this approach. She was only moderately attractive but there was something lubricious about her.

"I'm anxious to get to know the police in New York," she said. "I was wondering if you could be so kind as to introduce me to some policemen. Yes?" Well, sure, we could go for a walk and stop a police car and we could say ... No, that wasn't what she had in mind.

"Couldn't you take me to the precinct that covers the area where I live and let me meet the people in charge there?"

"What for?" I said, baffled.

"Oh," she said, "it would be nice to meet them, that's all. Your husband's a reporter and he would know how to introduce me properly." Perhaps that was how it was done in Amsterdam, newcomers dropping in to say hello to the gallant police. I didn't think such a custom, charming as it was, could be transplanted to Manhattan.

"Sure, any time," Tony said vaguely. "Give me a call. We'll see what we can do." I steered Tony away and that was that. For the time being, anyway.

At work, Fred Weintraub was busy saving Warner Brothers. In spite of the disapproving scowls of the hierarchy, in the days immediately preceding the Woodstock festival of peace and music in upstate New York—mud and music as it turned out—he handed the organizers thousands of dollars of Warner's money to subsidize the documentary film that was being planned to record the three days of the event. Previous rock documentaries had flopped. And this was Fred's first venture into movie making. It would be a financial disaster, said the suits. (The full story of Fred's role in the making of the film which won an Oscar and filled Warner's coffers can be found in his book, "Bruce Lee, Woodstock and Me".) It was the same story with his promotion of martial artist Bruce Lee who became a world-famous star until Lee's death.

In my neighborhood, I was discovering that Manhattan was in fact a series of villages. In our village there was Annette's Petit Veau, there was Gabby the butcher, also French, there was the Mayfair on First Avenue, where the models and the gays gathered, there was the A & P on the corner of our block, there was a fruit and produce stand on another, a shoe repairer, an antique store, a drug store, an ice cream store. I began to recognize people on the streets, even say hello to them. I still thought wistfully of home, particularly of Wales, but at the same time I was starting to feel like a real New Yorker.

There were hold-ups galore at the A & P. I was approaching the check-out counter one evening when a chap suddenly appeared with a pistol. There were at least two others, equally armed. Oooh, gangsters! Quickly, I kicked my handbag under the counter.

The gunman stuck his weapon in my ribs and ordered the manager to open the safe. What, now I was a hostage? Yes, I thought, open the damned safe and be quick about it. Why didn't he stick the gun in the manager's ribs? But the manager did as he was told and one of the robbers scooped up handfuls of cash. That was the strange time when customers paid with actual dollar bills.

"Open the till, gimme the money," said the first gunman to the checkout cashier.

She sighed, shook her head and calmly did as she was told. When I asked her later how she could take it all so casually she said, "Oh, I'm used to it. It happens all the time."

I was more excited. As the gang left, they warned, "No calls to the cops until we're well clear" but I made for the phone on the wall, dialed and was waiting for an answer when I felt something hard jammed against my head. It was a gun. Oh, not again. They had come back.

"I thought we told you not to call the fuckin' cops," said the gunman.

"I'm not calling them," I said. "I'm calling my fuckin' husband. He's a reporter with the Daily News."

"Okay," he said. "No fuckin' cops though." This time they left for good. All this happened half a block away from a police precinct on 51st St. Some cops came and questioned us. A detective friend of ours had once told us that the most important thing in identifying a miscreant was for witnesses to immediately be shown pictures of possible suspects.

"Take me to look at your pictures of suspects for this sort of thing," I said. "I got a good look at least one of them."

"We'll be in touch."

"No, right now while I remember what they looked like." It was no good. They left.

Six months later I got a call from a detective. "We want you to come and look at some pictures," he said. "See if you can recognize them for the A & P job."

"You must be joking," I said. "I've forgotten what they looked like ages ago." And that was that.

Our little third floor apartment was not exempt. Twice we were victims of burglars. The second time they used a crowbar to break open the peephole and reach in to find the lock. Among other stuff, they took some jewelry, probably quite valuable, that Tony's mother had given me. We called the cops and eventually one appeared, a charming young fellow who took extensive notes.

He examined the hole in the door. "Neat job," he said admiringly. "Very professional. See how he did it so he could reach in to get to the lock" Hang on. Whose side was he on?

"Fingerprints?" asked Detective Leonora.

"Er! Well, our print boys are pretty busy right now and he'd have used gloves. How long ago was the other break-in?"

"About four years ago," said Tony who had been in the apartment long before I moved in.

"Yeah, that's about the usual." He seemed pleased that our burglary supported his four year crime theory. How nice that we hadn't disturbed it. I was beyond dismayed. What was I going to say to Tony's mother? The cop was not hopeful about recovering the jewelry. His visit was pure public relations. Your police care about you. The brilliance of the show, "Seinfeld" was illustrated by an episode almost identical to ours in which Seinfeld, after answering lots of questions from a cop about a burglary, says, "We won't get anything back, will we?"

"Nah," says the cop.

Crime was all around us. On a day when Tony was again out of town, I got a call from the Dutch woman, Xaviera de Vries. She invited us to a party. When I told her that Tony was away, she said that I must come anyway, on my own. She was quite insistent. "You'll have a lovely time, meet interesting people," she said. For some reason I was suspicious and said I couldn't make it. The truth was that I didn't like her much. She sounded most disappointed. At this same period, I saw her escorting a gray-haired man, much older than her, into the modern, doorman building next to our little brownstone. What was that all about?

After Tony came back, he was sent to cover the hearings of the Knapp Commission which was investigating endemic corruption in the NYPD. Among the grubby tales that emerged the most riveting was that of a Manhattan plain clothed police officer, William Phillips, who for years had been taking payoffs from gamblers, hoods, businessmen and, most significant, a whorehouse madam. This madam was the one who finished off Phillips. Commission agents managed to make secret tapes of him discussing and taking payoffs from the madam who had gone on the pad to secure protection from arrest. The Commission turned Phillips and he went to work undercover for them in the hopes of a reduced sentence.

The first time the madam was mentioned she was identified only as Madam X but something about her description, the way she operated, alerted Tony. He knew this had to be Xaviera de Vries, the woman who wanted to be introduced to policemen. Of course, so that she could pay them off. The next day of the hearings, her name emerged, but now she was calling herself Xaviera Hollander, a play presumably on her country of origin. Perhaps she wanted to protect the sanctity of her family name. Goodness, that invitation to me to a party. Was she trying to recruit me into her stable? Was that a compliment or an insult?

Suddenly it all came together. An Australian friend of ours, Yvonne Dunleavy, the separated wife of a wild Aussi hack, had mentioned that she was writing a book about a whorehouse madam for book packager Robin Moore, the author of "The French Connection." Husband Steve passed into the lore of Manhattan night life when he was engaged in a romantic midnight interlude with a Swedish blonde in a snow bank outside Elaine's whose customers were crowded at the window watching fascinated. A snow plough came along and ran over one of Dunleavy's sprawled feet. Pete Hamill, much concerned, said, "I hope it wasn't his writing foot."

Through Yvonne, Tony was able to reach Xavera on the phone for his paper She was quite open about it all. "Yes, I'm Madam X," she said. "All this is so absurd. If they would only make it legal there would be no payoffs, no reason for protection. I provide a service. People come to me. You could call me a social worker. I'm not like the hooker on the street who has a pimp and robs people." She was outraged.

She said that the case which she tried to pay off ended with her being fined $100 for loitering for the purpose of prostitution. This was better than the original charge of promoting prostitution which would have made her liable to deportation, the thing she feared most.

"For the amount I paid (for the pad) I should have gone scot-free," she declared. "I don't mind paying protection but I should get value for money." She added that she was "inactive" because she was so busy writing her biography which would be called "The Happy Hooker In fact it was being written by Yvonne who was hard up at the time and, having split from Dunleavy, had nowhere to live.

The apartment below ours, normally occupied by a Sports Illustrated reporter, Lynn Simross, was empty because Lynn was out of town. She had gone to Florida for three months to learn how to train horses. I asked Yvonne if she would like to move into it, presuming Lynn was agreeable. She was. Thus it was that "The Happy Hooker" which would command the best-seller lists for months and make millions was written beneath our feet.

Moore was going to pay Yvonne $200 a week while she wrote the book but I told her, "You're crazy. Insist on a percentage of the profits so that if it's a hit you'll get a cut." She did and ended up with an apartment on Fifth Avenue, a delightful new husband and a house in the Hamptons. You owe me, Yvonne. Social worker Xaviera lasted in New York for another six months and then was deported.

She went with a certain style. Together with Yvonne, I rented a red double-decker London bus with the open platform at the rear which thousands, probably millions, of Londoners had used to jump off and on while the vehicle was still slowly moving. The bus, flaunting painted Union Jacks on its side, was battered and some of the seats had been removed but the engine still worked and a driver was included in the deal. We loaded it with hors d'oeuvres, beer, spirits and champagne for guests at Xaviera's farewell. She was being deported the next day. The idea was to drive around Manhattan while having a jolly time on board. It was the start of a really, really deplorable evening that I wouldn't have missed for anything.

The bus picked up the aggrieved hooker at her apartment. She was wearing a fur coat and a multi-colored dress with a hem high enough to double as a tunic. While photographers took pictures, we drove to Costello's, a hack hangout on Third Avenue with original murals by Thurber decorating the walls. Most of the guests were expat reporters who liked to call themselves hacks and their London papers "comics" to show ironically that they never took themselves or their papers seriously. Sometimes they reminded me of the lost generation created by Fitzgerald and Hemingway in the 1920s, but not often. As far as I could tell, there was no Gatsby or, God forbid, Jake Barnes among them but their signature tune might well have been "Ain't We Got Fun." In Costello's everybody but Xaviera loaded up with strong drink. The guest of honor, who could be puritanical at times, sipped orange juice. Xaviera didn't smoke or drink strong waters.

I had equipped myself with a whistle which I blew to signal it was time to move on. By this time the bus driver had learned the nature of the occasion and he balked. "I'm a good family man," he said, "and a follower of Muhammed's teachings. I can't take part in this debauchery." I thrust more money at him until it was enough to overcome his distaste. Anyway, Xaviera, after having pictures taken of her stalwart thighs, begged off because she had a lot of packing to do. I suspected that she didn't really approve of such public enjoyment.

Told that the moveable feast was heading for Umberto's Clam House in Little Italy where Crazy Joey Gallo had been murdered a couple of weeks earlier, she said, "The Mafiosi kill each other and nothing happens but I get thrown out of the country for providing a service." Perhaps she did have a point. She saw herself as a hard working businesswoman providing a service who had been taken advantage of by everybody she met.

No more do they make gangsters like Joey Gallo, aka Joey the Blond. Crazy Joe was reputed to keep a lioness in the basement of his home. Fond of black shirts and black suits, he liked to model himself on Richard Widmark who, playing a movie hoodlum, pushed a helpless old woman down a flight of stairs. Something of an insurgent in the Mob, Gallo complained that he was not being paid enough for his activities as a hit man and enforcer. What also got up the noses of the old time Mafiosi was his well-publicized and unlikely arrival among the chic sophisticates of Manhattan with whom he liked to discuss Dostoyevsky and Camus. The highbrow literati were fascinated by this real life gangster and he was fascinated by them. Crazy Joe even talked about writing a book about his life, maybe making a film which, to Mob bosses obsessed by secrecy, was even worse.

It all ended when his gangster enemies spotted him eating at 4 a.m. in Umberto's after a night on the town to celebrate his birthday. A team of four hit men was summoned. They burst into Umberto's where Crazy Joe was sitting facing a wall, a great mistake The hit men were not very good shots but they managed to put one bullet in their target's back, together with one or two in his backside. Crazy Joe, trying to draw his weapon, staggered out and collapsed in the street in a pool of blood. His bodyguard was wounded.

Without Xaviera the festivities took a vulgar turn. It was not in the best of taste, we had to admit, to wine and dine at Umberto's simply because a hoodlum had been murdered there but that was the point. A group celebrating the deportation of a madam would hardly have been welcome at the Plaza.

There were problems though in getting to Little Italy. The double-decker bus could not pass under some of Manhattan's bridges and had to detour all over the East Side which allowed the hacks on board to make deep inroads into the liquor supplies being served on the lower deck by a veteran bartender from Costello's.

Obviously concerned about the increasing merriment developing behind him, the bus driver became even more disenchanted. "I'm a follower of Muhammed and I cannot . . ."

"I know, I know," I said and pushed more money at him, enough to persuade him to continue. But to express his emotions he accelerated, swinging around the turns like a crazed NASCAR driver. I blew my whistle but he wouldn't slow down. It was astonishing that we didn't hear police sirens. Where were the police when you didn't want them? As we swirled around one corner, the hors d'oeuvres, prettily arranged on a table next to the drinks, went hurtling out of an open window. Nobody seemed to care much, not so long as the liquor was safe.

Thus we wended our way downtown to Umberto's. Things were now getting out of hand. In the restaurant, where the bullet holes had been plastered over, a silly Brit thought it would be funny to whip away a chair just as another guest, Australian hack Derryn Hinch, was about to occupy it. Derryn, a great friend of ours, fell on his bottom and the heavy chair went over on to the floor with a loud crack. The waiters, gun shy after the fusillade that wasted Joey Gallo, hit the floor. A furious altercation broke out between the two guests involved in the chair upheaval. (A year or so later, the silly Brit ended up in a front office in Hollywood which was where he belonged). Outside, angry mothers were leaning out of their windows shouting that the bus was spouting fumes and engine noise keeping their children awake because the driver wouldn't turn off the engine, saying that he might not be able to start it again. He went to the bathroom.

Juliet, a willowy English beauty, climbed into the driver's seat and tried to drive off but she couldn't get the gears to engage. When the driver returned, she sulkily climbed down at his insistence, saying she had just wanted to try it out with a spin around the block. The mothers in the surrounding tenements were still screaming about the noise and fumes.

Signor Umberto said we should leave as soon as possible. His regular customers didn't like being stared at by these uptown guests as if they were exotic flora and fauna. "It makes them nervous, see. They get indigestion." I think he was also offended that some of the more crass members of the party had demanded unsuccessfully that they be seated at the table where Crazy Joe was whacked. "It's in bad taste," said the restaurateur.

Finally, I blew my whistle and we all climbed back on the bus where more money was stuffed into the driver's hand and we chugged uptown. Along the way, Big Mike, an American hack who found the expats interesting, slipped while climbing down the stairs and put his elbow through the large back window. Down with the glass came the last straw. Now we would have to pay for the window repair on top of everything else. I was so exasperated I spun him towards the open door and pushed. Big Mike weighed at least twice my poundage but such was the force of my irritation that he tumbled out. "Hey," was all he could say before he vanished into the night somewhere in the E.20s.

The entire episode, I thought, illustrated Scott Fitzgerald's description of New York as a place with a "racy, adventurous feel." I couldn't have said it better and I didn't.

The evening ended at Yvonne's apartment on E.58th St. Two New York City policemen arrived, saying that somebody had invited them, they couldn't quite remember who. Easing their gun holsters into a more comfortable position, they sat and sipped Scotch with beer chasers and said nobody would miss them because they were on their "lunch hour." Their lunch hour lasted until dawn.

Thank goodness Xaviera wasn't present for all this. She had her standards and she would have been pained by the behavior of all concerned. As for me, most peculiarly I found the evening had resulted in my warming even more to America. Clearly, this was a country where weird things could and did happen.

CHAPTER SIX

As I suppose in all marriages, there were some pot holes along the way, such as my birthday. All I got was a birthday card as Tony rushed off to work. "I'll call you," he said over his shoulder. I was going to give him the Fairclough glare but he had gone. I spent the day fighting off the sulks and considered abandoning Tony in favor of drinks with some of my work-mates. When he called me, he got a cool reception. "Meet me at six, at the corner of 42nd and Second," he said. "It will be more convenient for where we're going. We'll have dinner, just the two of us." Yes, more convenient for him, just across the road from the Daily News building. Hah. Dinner wouldn't cut it. I punished him by arriving fifteen minutes late.

When I showed up he immediately hailed a cab. Before he climbed in he muttered something to the driver through the open window and off we went. I gave him the chilly treatment until I noticed we were heading east out of Manhattan and into Queens. "What the hell . . ." He smirked and said, "Wait a bit. We'll soon be there." There, it turned out, was La Guardia airport. He escorted me to the Eastern Airlines shuttle and from the signs I realized we were heading for Boston. Intriguing. After we landed, Tony found a taxi and whispered something to the driver. Off we went, through the tunnel, and into downtown Boston. "What the hell . . ." We arrived outside a restaurant with a modestly handsome facade standing in a little street that was more like an alley. He led me inside. "Locke-Ober," he said. "Supposed to be great. We have a reservation. Happy birthday." Inside it was unpretentiously elegant, with the buzz of Boston accents and an atmosphere that said it took food seriously. It had been there for ever and, as we discovered, the food was first rate. So was the wine. It was the sort of place where you could imagine the Kennedys plotting over their lobster thermidor. There were a few other women diners but, with its shining paneling and scent of expensive cigars, it had the feeling of a men's club. The waiters, wearing long white aprons which brushed the floor, were solemn as befitted a temple of cuisine, none of that ridiculous introduction, "My name is Peter and I shall be your waiter tonight." Our waiter was as formal as a bishop but relaxed enough to give me a smile. Settled in and enjoying my Dover sole, I decided to forgive Tony for his unforgiveable behavior.

The trouble was that we lingered too long at Locke-Ober and when we reluctantly left it was late, too late for the last Eastern shuttle flight back to La Guardia. We inquired at the counter and found that American Airlines had a regular flight into Kennedy Airport. Passengers were boarding and it was scheduled to leave in ten minutes. "Er, listen, darling," said Tony looking suitably embarrassed. "D'you have any money? I knew Locke-Ober would be expensive but not that expensive. That wine . . . It seems a regular flight costs a bit more than the shuttle. More than I've got actually."

"Where's your check book?"

"At home."

"Idiot."

"Where's yours?"

"That's beside the point. You're the host." In those days, neither of us had credit cards.

I sighed and hunted through my purse until I found enough cash to make up the difference and satisfy the agent behind the counter. "You'd better hurry," he said. At Kennedy we had to find more cash for the cab but finally, just about broke, we made it back to Manhattan.

Here's the thing about the ups and downs of adventures, big or small, dramatic or risible: they are memorable. If all runs smoothly they are soon forgotten. And the Dover sole had been exceptional.

It was Tony's birthday three months later so I decided I would equal his surprise jaunt to Boston. Unknown to him, I invited a bunch of friends to a party in our little two-and-a-half room apartment on 51st St. He was surprised but so was I. A number of the guests had not been invited. At its peak, there were more than 40 people jammed into the meager space and the noise was shattering. It was a tribute to the long-ago work of the builders that the floor didn't collapse. Among those present was man-about-town Anthony Haden-Guest who frequently claimed he was the model for the louche English reporter in Tom Wolfe's "Bonfire of the Vanities." When I confronted him to ask why he was there when he hadn't been invited he said in his debonair fashion, "Oh, I knew you'd want me to attend the gathering. No party's a real success unless I'm there."

I was in the bathroom, trying to recover the splendid birthday cake which somebody had dumped in the lavatory bowl, when a fight broke out. It was Steve Dunleavy and Big Mike of course, the macho nuisances. They were always fighting. Tony was furious. Protesting, "Hey, this is my birthday party, you bastards," he charged in to separate the combatants. He succeeded in breaking it up and neither Dunleavy nor Big Mike was hurt, but Tony was. He got a black eye. After that, the party-goers drifted away. Actually, as I discovered the next morning, the eye wasn't black. It was an interesting mix of colors including yellow and purple. You live and learn. Black eyes aren't black, they're more a rainbow.

At work at Warner's, I was making some American friends. One was Bob Jiras, or B.J., a veteran Hollywood makeup artist who had created the first makeup department for CBS TV before moving on to work on scores of films. Among the actors whose features he had enhanced were Elizabeth Taylor, Warren Beatty, Paul Newman, Natalie Wood and on and on. He had worked on scores of films, from "Bonnie and Clyde," "The Hustler", "McCabe and Mrs. Miller to "Ishtar" and something called "Hey, Let's Twist" that he didn't talk about much. He was consumed by the movie business but now he wanted to move up and become a director. In pursuit of this unlikely goal he spent time hanging around my office hoping to arouse interest among any Warner executives he could approach or, better still, find the money to make a film called "The Hanged Man." Nobody bit.

He was a tall, lugubrious featured chap with spaniel eyes who nonetheless could laugh at himself and the absurdities of show business. After a while he gave up but we remained in touch. Then he called to say that lightning had struck. He had the money and he had the cast and crew to make a movie to be called "I Am The Cheese" based on a novel of that name written by his friend, Robert Cormier The book was a subtle tale of a teenage boy caught in a web of government conspiracy, skillfully written but not easy to follow without considerable concentration. B.J. was producing it as well as directing. His stars amounted to B.J.'s repertory company. One of the key roles was played by Hope Lange whose sister was married to B.J. Hope Lange had been married to Don Murray who had another role. Another actor was Robert Wagner who was, oh, that's enough of that.

Our theory was that, out of affection for B.J., financial backing had come from one or more Hollywood stars and the cast was working for the minimum. The author, Cormier, had a part. Still, good films had been made with small budgets. The movie was to be filmed in Vermont and Tony and I were invited to visit the set. We couldn't make it but at one point during the filming B.J. took a break and met us in New York.

"You know," he said, "the amazing thing is how easy I'm finding this directing gig. It's going so smoothly it's like a dream. I don't know what the fuss is all about. Just so easy."

We didn't say anything but neither of us liked the sound of that. Directing a film wasn't supposed to be easy. Surely it demanded a vivid imagination, years of experience behind the camera. It was complicated and painfully difficult; having to deal with everything from cranky stars to catering for the crew's refined palates.

"I Am The Cheese" was a flop. The reviews were unkind and one in an important national paper was scathing. The critic seemed to be insulted that he had been forced to waste his precious time on this trash and he went on from there at length. Now that B.J. has gone I can tell the truth which is that it was not very good. It was confused and, as a result, at times boring. But surely it would have been better for reviewers to ignore it if they felt it was so bad. Or it would have been lovely if they had been a little less venomous. I know, I know, their duty is to the reader who might think of going to see it. Sorry, to me that's pure cant. The writers wanted to demonstrate how ferociously clever they could be.

Now I don't think these critics broke B.J. But when we went to visit him later at his home in Vermont he was a different man. He had reached for film glory and fallen miserably short. We didn't talk about his film. What could you say? But the spark had left him. He died in his beloved Vermont in 2000.

Words can wound. Successful writers, artists, directors, I thought, were fair game for tough criticism. The unsuccessful, the struggling, not so much.

Tony had started writing books, so we had a little extra money trickling into the bank. We talked about a place in the country to get away from Manhattan at weekends. I thought a farmhouse in Connecticut would be nice. Blazes in the fireplace while the snow drifted silently down outside. In the spring, sitting on the deck at cocktail time watching the sun set. In the summer, dips in the river I imagined flowing past the farmhouse. Visiting friends admiring the brilliance of autumn leaves and enjoying the crisp air.

There was a problem . . . well, two actually. For a mortgage, we learned we would need a credit rating and, although we didn't owe a cent, we didn't have one. Nor did we have a credit card. And we didn't really have much money. Then Tony remembered that on a visit to Ray Miles in St. Thomas some years back he had found himself with spare cash and had bought a quarter of an acre of beach front land with the vague idea of building a house. There was no sandy beach, just shingles and rocks, but still . . .

He called the real estate bloke who had handled the sale and he promised to see if he could find a buyer. He called back to say he had, a woman who was very excited about the bit of land overlooking the sea even though it was on the unfashionable end of the island. She, not Tony, planned to build a house. The deal was done.

I got a credit card and immediately went to Macy's where I spent furiously and enjoyably, thus in the strange American fashion proving that because we owed money I was credit worthy. Now it was just a question of finding the perfect Connecticut farmhouse.

Instead, we found ourselves examining an isolated little house on a wooded hillside outside Woodstock, N.Y. It looked like a hunting lodge. It had thick stone walls, a big fireplace and it came with 28 acres of trees and rocks on land steep enough to delight a mountain goat. No river to swim in although the house was built with river stone. No deck from which to take in the scenery. We loved it. Our real estate agent in Woodstock, the chubby, comfortably rumpled Mr. Schultz whom we called Schultzy seemed to take a liking to this odd couple of aliens who talked funny and he volunteered to personally guarantee a mortgage with the local bank.

The date for moving in was set at March 1st. We couldn't wait. Armed with the key we arrived on the last evening of February, smelled the clean, pine scented air, built a fire and settled in, not bothered that, except for a long picnic table, there was no furniture. It was the first time either of us had owned a home. Outside the night was black as it never was in Manhattan or London. There was no sound except for the rustling of night creatures in the woods. Good, another adventure.

When we woke in the morning there was a peculiar glow coming through the windows. Peering out we saw that a foot of snow had fallen while we slept. It was beautiful, crisp and clean. We also saw that somebody on a tractor with a plough was down at the end of the slope of the driveway digging out our little Volkswagen, bought from Lynn Simross, ageing and dented but still serviceable. We had left it outside the little shed at the bottom of the driveway the night before. I put on some boots, threw a coat over my night dress and rushed down to say hello. That was how we met our neighbor, Nestor Bryant, who became one of our very best friends, one who, in a reversal of initial feelings, helped me recognize the generosity and humanity of so many ordinary Americans.

CHAPTER SEVEN

Nestor ploughed the entire length of the driveway. His acreage adjoined ours and from our new country home, if the trees were bare, we could just make out the roof of his house alongside a pretty swimming pool. He worked for IBM in Kingston, 20 minutes east of Woodstock, and in his off-work hours ran a tractor sales and repair shop.

He was my first real American pal in the sense that he didn't mix with the sophisticates of Manhattan who produced nothing but words or pictures. A Republican, he wouldn't object to being included in Nixon's silent majority.

Nestor Bryant was a chunky, bespectacled chap with a ready laugh who, it seemed, could turn his hand to anything. He was the perfect neighbor. During our week-day absences, he kept an eye on our house and when things went wrong he was always able to fix the problem. It was like having an unpaid caretaker. Before driving back to the city, we would leave a red light bulb burning in the window where Nestor could see it. It was somehow rigged so that if it went out, it meant that the furnace had stopped heating the house. Water pipes would freeze solid. Using a key we had given him, Nestor would go over and take care of the crisis.

During the bitter upstate winters the pipeline from the outside oil tank to the burner would freeze and he would spend hours in the ferocious cold thawing it with a blow torch until, finally, we buried the tank so that the pipeline was underground and protected from the cold. He gave us a good price on a specially designed tractor with six wheels that could navigate the tricky downhill sections above the meadow that skirted the road. At weekends, Tony would ride it up and down, pretending to be a country gentleman while I did more important things like tackling the Saturday Times crossword, pretending to be an intellectual. Volunteering his services, Nestor deftly repaired a long dining table from which a section had come adrift. We still use it.

We would shop in Woodstock and found the town to be an interesting mix. On one side were weekenders, musicians and hippies, waiting for daddy's check, many attracted to the town because of its name although the Woodstock festival had been held miles away at Bethel. On the other were long-resident blue-collar workers of the Republican stripe. Often, the village green would be occupied by one or two hairy young men playing guitars, presumably letting arriving hipsters know they had come to the right funky place. It was a tolerant, free-wheeling town and they all seemed to get on well enough. The area was served by an old-fashioned weekly newspaper, the Ulster County Townsman, which concentrated on births, weddings, funerals and the vacations of the locals. After we arrived on the scene, a group of newcomers launched another more professional weekly, the Woodstock Times, which became so successful that it split into two sections. Neither paper promoted any particular political view. Both papers survive today.

One of Nestor's daughters, pre-teen Holly, thought us interesting enough to wander over for consultations about the difficulties of growing up. Nestor and his wife, Joan, would come for dinner on Saturday nights and play poker for minor sums. Also usually at the table would be a group of British or Australian journalists and their ladies, even the occasional American, invited up for the weekend. Alcohol was consumed of course but, surprisingly, not a torrent because many of the guests were at Woodstock sucking up fresh air to recover from their week-day debaucheries in smoke clouded bars. The meeting of the two cultures was interesting to watch.

An English hack who aspired to be hip, Dermot, came one weekend in distressed blue jeans with carefully designed rips down the leg through which his beefy legs could be spied, then the ultra of expensive high fashion in the city. Dermot, a deftly ironic writer, had only one eye. If questioned about his missing orb he would say he lost it as a youngster when hit by a cricket ball. That answer would come early in the evening. Later, after a number of drinks, he might change it slightly, claiming that he was gored while fighting not one bull but two in Seville. He also lost a glass eye while swimming in the Hamptons. Asked to admire Dermot's jeans, Nestor couldn't believe that somebody would pay handsomely for a tattered garment that he would have thrown away as worn out.

In turn, the cosmopolitan city folks gazed at Nestor as if he were an exotic jungle flower. The chap actually worked with his hands and was definitely right of center in a country already to the right. But eventually they were beguiled by this country bumpkin who turned out to be witty, knowledgeable and always ready to laugh at their worst jokes as well as being a player to watch out for at the poker table, even if he didn't understand the importance of torn jeans.

In the summer, Sunday afternoons would often be spent at the Bryants' swimming pool. Little Holly from next door grew and grew until she was in her mid-teens. One afternoon as we lolled around the pool in the hot sun reading the Sunday papers I noticed that a couple of my guests, Brits of course, were staring as if mesmerized towards the far end of the pool. I followed their gaze and saw that Holly and a couple of her teeny-bopper friends were sitting with their feet dangling in the water. They were wearing tight jeans and they were casually dipping their hands into the pool and splashing water on to their slim blue thighs which gleamed alluringly in the sunshine. I was pretty sure the young things knew exactly what effect they were having on the adult watchers who weren't licking their lips but looked as if they were about to.

I coughed meaningfully toward them and raised a disapproving eyebrow. They hastily retreated behind their newspapers.

The pool was the scene of another sexually charged incident. Adam, one of our frequent guests, was a tall, languid Englishman with social pretensions who said he was a free lance journalist although it was never clear to me that he ever spent time actually working. He arrived this time with an attractive woman, American and, according to Adam, an heiress. An heiress to what? Adam didn't know but the important thing was that she was an heiress It was very hot and as we all sat around on the lawn immediately outside the house after lunch, she asked if anybody objected if she took off her T-shirt and went topless. We didn't object so off it came. Miaow, miaow! There wasn't much for our visiting lechers to enjoy. She had the figure of a boy. But it was noticeable that she had a mole dead center between her tiny breasts.

She immediately won the title, "Triple Nipple."

When we all wandered across Nestor's field to the pool, she put her T-shirt back on. We found Joan established poolside and the heiress asked if she would mind her going topless in the lovely sunshine. Joan was a prim lady, not used to worldly ways, and this was church-going, God-fearing upstate New York not the decadent French Riviera, but she was so startled at the idea she responded with a muttered acquiescence.

Off again came the T-shirt. At this point, Nestor was a short distance away mowing his grass. He glanced over at us and when he saw Triple Nipple's state of undress as she lay in a lounge chair he nearly fell off his tractor. Recovering, he swiftly joined us for a chat, showing a friendly interest in the heiress and, more particularly, her nipples. Joan was not amused and I don't think the episode did their marriage much good. Indeed, I've often wondered if the invasion of foreign outsiders so different to country folk was at least partly responsible for the eventual break-up of the Bryant marriage. For break-up they did. Nestor was expelled from his beloved property and went to live in a mobile home while Joan remained.

Another weekend when Adam was in residence, a young English woman on the loose, Wendy, joined us. She also was a free-lance hack, with a care-free attitude towards work. Over dinner, she said that she was working on an article for the BBC magazine, had all the material but couldn't settle down to actually writing the piece. Writer's block.

"Hey, Adam," she said, "how about you writing the article with the material I'll give you. We'll split the fee 50-50."

"Certainly," said Adam, always hard up. "But can't you give me a better percentage since I'll be doing all the work?"

"No," said Wendy.

That was the start of a long and tedious argument over the following days with Wendy arguing that lazy Adam had done a sloppy job that would not be acceptable in London while Adam said he had done his usual brilliant job and lazy Wendy just didn't want to pay up. I don't know and don't care how it was sorted out but I do know that when Adam was at Woodstock things could get out of hand. Hang on. Wasn't I entertaining the belief that Brit beliefs and culture were superior?

One of our dearest friends was Lana Wells, an Australian writer married to Derryn Hinch, the hard-thrusting Aussie hack of Umberto's infamy. They visited Woodstock frequently and Lana came to love the place so much that she wrote a column about it for her paper, the Melbourne Herald and worked on an oil-painting of the house in the snow which hangs in our home today.

Sadly, she split with Derryn and returned to Australia. There she married again and eventually contacted us to say she and her new husband would be visiting the States and would love to spend a day or two at Woodstock. Of course. We knew how much it meant to her.

Just before the weekend when the couple was expected, Adam reached us and said he planned to come up with a couple of friends. Okay? Foolishly, we agreed to receive them. All welcome at Hospitality Hall. Lana and her chap arrived first and she happily showed him around the house and property, telling him stories of past fun and games. He was a nice enough fellow but a bit stiff and formal, un-Australian in fact, perhaps feeling uncomfortable at this introduction to a part of Lana's life before he married her. Then Adam and his friends, two women, drove up. Straight away it seemed to us that the trio was under the influence of something. The women were dreadful, unpleasant, giggling together, ignoring us, acting like trollops.

The weekend became a disaster. These guests did not mix, did not want to. The warm atmosphere of the house turned icy. Lana tried to hide her dismay but we could tell she was deeply upset at their behavior which was ruining her memory of a beloved place. Her husband became even more stilted. We felt helpless. Looking back, I think now we should have ordered Adam to take his horrible women away but it probably wouldn't have helped. The damage was done. Lana and her chap left early the next morning. If Woodstock was the silver lining to our lives up to that point I would have to say that every silver lining has a cloud. The bimbos left without a word of thanks for their drinks and dinner.

I shouldn't be too hard on Adam; he could be funny and charming. He once told the story of how he managed to reject formal religion against the wishes of his family which trooped off to church every Sunday morning. His father, a London judge, expected Adam to attend with the rest but at 16, Adam decided he had had enough of the kneeling and praying and singing every week. When he told his father that he no longer wished to be a party to it, his papa, as if sitting on the bench looking down at a barrister for the defense, became judicial and laid out his terms for accepting Adam's negative point of view regarding church-going.

Adam's arguments would have to be rational, logical, unemotional and so persuasive that they would be impervious to attack, he ruled. Acknowledging family ties, the judge did not don a robe or wig for the occasion.

Adam claimed that his words were so effective that with hardly any time spent considering his verdict, that judge announced that the youngster had spoken well and would no longer be expected to attend Sunday services. At least that was Adam's story.

When the twins arrived on the Woodstock scene, Nestor immediately fell for them. He started talking about the future when he would take them fishing in the local ponds. I think he had a Tom Sawyer vision of the boys sitting quietly at the pond with him, talking about life while watching their fishing lines and chewing on a bit of straw. Indeed the boys did develop a fascination with water. They liked to go to the Woodstock library, but not for the books. A few yards away from the library was a stream and they loved to throw stones into the water, chortling with joy when they made a really good splash. The little horrors could do it for hours. Who needed television which in Woodstock we didn't have?

At last, when they were two or three, Nestor realized his ambition to take them fishing. He provided them with cheap rods and took them to a pretty little pond, fringed with rushes and with nobody else around. It was cupped in a valley surrounded by wooded hills. Perfect. But it didn't work out well. Nestor showed them how to hold the rods and cast the bait.

"Now we sit and wait," he said. The twins were far too energetic to just sit watching the water. They were more Huckleberry Finn than Tom Sawyer. They wanted to throw stones at the water, not just stare at it. Nestor persisted on his own and in fact hauled in a fish. They graciously admired it but that was it, the end of Nestor's vision of bucolic bliss. Poor Nestor.

In New York, Tony and I were astonished to find ourselves fixated on an American sport. We both were Rugby fans, me of Newport and, of course, the Welsh national team. So, of all things, how could we possibly become entranced by baseball, in particular as played by the Yankees? In the U.K. little girls played rounders which, I gathered, was the gentle ancestor of American baseball.

The answer was Billy Martin, the manager, and players like Reggie Jackson, catcher Thurman Munson with the gunfighter mustache, Sparky Lyall, Catfish Hunter, Goose Gossage. Oh, what lovely names. These were characters with a capital C, inhabiting what became known as the Bronx Zoo. Billy Martin, who looked like a tapped-out riverboat gambler, seethed like an unexploded bomb and was in the running for world champion saloon fighter. Thurman Munson was said to be moody, but a contrarian team-mate commented that the adjective didn't fit, "If you're moody that means you're nice some of the time," he said. Was Hunter christened Catfish? Gossage baptized Goose?. When they were at the ballpark, it wasn't just a matter of one player heaving a ball at another player wielding a bat over and over. It was better than any circus. You never knew when fights would erupt in the dugout or Billy, who liked his drink as much as he liked baseball, maybe more, would scream at an official while kicking dirt on his shoes or call Jackson a born liar and the owner, George Steinbrenner, a felon because the owner had been found guilty of illegally contributing cash for the campaign of my old friend, Richard Nixon. Steinbrenner had developed an interesting habit of firing Billy before hiring him again.

It was, I realized later, part of the Americanization of Leonora. As much as we loved Rugby, it had nothing to compare with this. It was like a soap opera on steroids directed by Billy Wilder. Baseball purists might have despised the constant hullabaloo but I relished every moment.

Billy Martin, the owner and the players were unique and we watched them because they were unique and we felt we knew them and along the way I learned something about baseball and about the country. I began to understand the bunt and the fly-ball although I had trouble with the suicide squeeze.

This was a time when New York City was in a sad state, none of it worse than the Bronx which looked something like Dresden in 1946. Behind Yankee Stadium was the South Bronx which was commanded by poverty, crime, drugs, arsonists and despair. Presidential candidates would come to inspect it, shake their heads and tell the cameras that something had to be done, then go away and do nothing. Addicts would shoot up in abandoned buildings and torch them although cynics suggested cash-hungry landlords might not be above hiring arsonists to do the job before applying for insurance benefits.

It was so bad that TV cameras at one game caught flames leaping from a building just beyond the ball park and the commentator, one Howard Cosell, declared, "Ladies and gentlemen, the Bronx is burning." The game, of course, continued. For drama you couldn't beat it. One thing baffled me, though. This was the second game of the World Series. World Series? The only teams were American, although one or two Canadian teams stocked with Americans sometimes hovered on the fringes. One dubious reason I heard for the suggestion that the entire planet competed was that the first series had been sponsored by a newspaper, the New York World. That surely was stretching. More likely the exaggeration was typical of blowhard Americans who believed the whole world revolved around them.

A couple of years later, Munson was killed in the crash of his private plane. As these remarkable characters faded away, so did our interest in baseball. Their places were taken by bland players and managers who wouldn't think of calling the owner a criminal. Today I can hardly name a big-time player.

Towards the end of the season, I became pregnant with the twins although neither George Steinbrenner nor his Yankees had anything to do with it. Robert would later claim he was senior because he arrived five minutes before David.

In Tony's absence on a story and anxious that the boys would be able to claim British citizenship, I took them to the British Consulate to register their births. I was infuriated to learn that the male-dominated U.K. had decreed that only the father could register the children.

"That's crazy," I protested. "I'm the mother, I gave birth to them. He didn't."

At the hospital, Beth Israel in Manhattan, they allowed only the mother, not the father, to take new-borns out of the hospital on the grounds that the nurses knew exactly who the mother was but not who the father was. "The father could be anybody," one tactless nurse told me. "Sometimes not even the mother knows who the father is." When I pointed this out at the consulate I got the answer, "Rules are rules." Where had I heard that one before? Oh, right, the British Virgin Islands. Hmm, just two contacts with British officialdom abroad, neither good.

Finally, Tony returned. He went to the consulate with identification documents and persuaded the bureaucrats that he was satisfactorily male. The boys were registered. But I was so angry that I wouldn't leave it at that. I later described what had happened to a good friend of Tony's, the editor of the London Daily Mail, David English, who was visiting New York.

English, later Sir David, the Golden Boy of the U.K.'s popular press, was professionally close to Margaret Thatcher who had just been elected the first woman prime minister of the U.K. and was about to launch a series of slashing right-wing reforms aimed at dragging Britain into a more and more competitive world. English used to pop around to Downing Street after he had put his paper to bed to share a sandwich and chat with the Valkyrie-like prime minister. English had been dismayed by my treatment and he raised the matter with Thatcher

In 1981, a couple of years later, the discriminatory rule suddenly no longer was a rule. The convoluted and legalistic word ordered by parliament went out from London to British embassies and consulates around the world that the mother of a child could register the little darling without the father's appearance.

English is dead now and Thatcher is sick with dementia, her memory in tatters, so I cannot swear that I was responsible for this policy change. But wouldn't it be pretty to think so?

Maggie Thatcher was no feminist and neither was I. At home and at school, I had been raised to believe that I was as worthy as any male and could take them on in any sphere. I never felt victimized because of my gender. I didn't care about the notorious glass ceiling because I believed life was for enjoyment, not for an all-consuming struggle to the top. Where was the fun in that? Women who wanted to reach for the sky should do what Thatcher did to her Conservative Party leader and rival, Ted Heath: Stop marching and waving banners and slip a dagger through any male ribs in the way or if that didn't work put on some especially seductive perfume and try a stab in the back. As demonstrated in the matter of our marriage license, tears can be highly effective, too.

The issue of women's rights emerged at work at Warner's. My boss, Fred Weintraub, fell victim to his rival in Hollywood, John Calley, who persuaded the hierarchy that Fred should be shipped to the West Coast where, of course, Calley could keep an eye on him. His office was dismantled and we were told to get rid of his furniture from the set of My Fair Lady. To help out, I volunteered to get rid of a large tapestry and a gorgeous leather couch which I installed in our apartment.

With Fred gone, I was moved to a new enterprise launched by the ever expanding Steve Ross. In one big deal, Ross found that in addition to his main target, he was becoming the owner of five radio stations around the country. To win FCC approval of his ownership he had to submit a report on the programs he would introduce and on the public's opinion of the stations. I was dispatched to three of the stations, in Florida, Chicago and Harlem to gather facts for the submission to the FCC. In Florida and Chicago I got a glimpse of the country vastly different to Manhattan. The third station in Harlem was closer to home. I wandered the streets asking anybody I met what they thought of the station and taking careful notes. At one point, I went into a bodega and in conversation with the man behind the counter asked what his most popular sales item was.

"Oh, SOS and Brillo steel wool," he said.

"Your customers must be determined to keep their homes nice and clean."

"It's not that," he said. "They use the steel wool to jam into holes in the wall to keep out the rats."

"That's brilliant," I declared. "Would they work for mouse holes?" We had a couple of holes near the floor in the kitchen wall but I thought, and hoped, they were too small for rats.

The bodega bloke shrugged and said, "Perhaps. I don't know."

I bought some. But the mice still kept leaving evidence of their invasion. Perhaps tough New York mice had become used to eating steel wool.

Next I was switched to the Warner Books publishing company which was commanded by a talented but diminutive executive whom, employing my antic imagination, I privately thought of as Mr. Titch. I mention his stature because I came to believe that later it might have affected my future.

One of my first tasks in the publishing world was to work on a coffee-table book revolving around the exploits of the comic character, Wonder Woman. Feminist icons like Gloria Steinem, Dr. Phyllis Chessler and Bea Fietler were leading the charge but I didn't have much contact with them. My task was to help sort through the thousands of Wonder Woman comics and select suitable ones for the book. The mistake I made came when a group of us led by Mr. Titch was about to enter an elevator. I held the door open in such a way that to enter Mr. Titch had to walk under my outstretched arm. "In you go," I chirped as if he were a small pet. As he passed under the arm, he looked up and gave me a sulfurous look that remains with me today. I didn't last long at Warner Books.

Whether it was punishment or reward I don't know, but I was appointed publisher of Coronet Magazine which had come under Steve Ross's control. I knew nothing about magazines or journalism in general but I learned that I was responsible for its, and my, future. Now my head was butting against the glass ceiling, if there was such a thing, and I feared that the result would be a bloody scalp. I also knew that Coronet Magazine was gasping for life. In fact it was in such a bad financial way that it had stopped publishing, although nobody seemed to have noticed. Now we were about to re-launch it as a magazine for women, give it one more chance. Lucky me.

Who did I know who could help? Why Yvonne Dunleavy, author of the "The Happy Hooker," of course. Yvonne was an experienced journalist as well as something of an expert on running a house of ill repute like Coronet magazine because of her research with the happy hooker so she was well qualified. She came on board as editor and we went to work. One of the first things we discovered was that Coronet had some mysterious connection to a warehouse in New Jersey. We went out there and discovered it was packed with thousands of items ranging from soap to table cloths to cereals. Weird.

We made inquiries and discovered that, in its previous incarnation, Coronet had developed a system with advertisers who did not want to pay with hard cash. Instead they shipped an agreed amount of the goods that they manufactured to the New Jersey warehouse. The secret of what the previous regime planned to do with all this stuff remained hidden.

I found that with Yvonne highly capable of running the editorial side my main role was to persuade companies we were a much more attractive advertising medium than Ladies Home Journal or Time magazine. I had little success. The general response of potential advertisers was, "Coronet? What the hell is that?"

In most editions the only ads were placed by Warner's which of course owned the damn magazine. Still, the ad for "Deliverance" with Jon Voight and Burt Reynolds looked good on the back cover. Made by Warner Bros. of course. Then there were Smokey the Bear and March of Dimes though of course they were public service ads. Another good one was an ad for a touching story about an autistic little boy, called "A Child Called Noah." It was published by Warner Paperback Library, one of Mr. Titch's helpful contributions. Oh, and we had a professionally laid out ad for Parliament cigarettes. "It works like a cigarette holder works."

Yvonne did a good professional job, filling the pages with articles, horoscopes, recipes and book excerpts. Not from "The Happy Hooker." Georgette Heyer was more our style and a lot cheaper. We even had a West Coast editor, Joanne Carson, one of Johnny's wives. In the February, 1973, edition Yvonne ran an article about exercises for the eyes and I showed my dedication to the magazine by modeling various eye exercises for a photographer. I looked weird. Would you catch Vogue magazine's editor in chief Anna Wintour, aka Nuclear Wintour, doing that? I don't think so.

Still it swiftly became clear that Ladies Home Journal had nothing to fear from us. I was forced to call in Phil, our advertising manager, and fire him. He was affronted.

"You should be fired yourself," he declared. "And I should be the publisher." Maybe he was right.

The inevitable happened and after about a year the magazine was closed for the second time and I was out of Warner's for good. It must have cost them a lot but with money flowing in from so many successful enterprises it was probably pocket money to Warner's and Steve Ross.

That difficulty with my career was equaled by the night Tony invited famous war correspondent Homer Bigart to dinner at our tiny apartment. It became known ever after as the Bigart Botch. Homer, a rumpled teddy bear of a man then working for the Times, had won two Pulitzer Prizes for his war coverage starting in World War 11 and including just about every succeeding American war. He had a charming little stutter that somehow made you listen more closely to him. I liked him partly because he said he loved London where he had worked during the German blitz. He and Tony had met on an out-of-town story and a jolly night of war stories was anticipated. Instead, here came trouble. First, our air conditioner broke down and it was one of the hottest nights of the summer. Second, something went wrong around the stove and the dinner I cooked was a disaster, almost uneatable. We should have said, to hell with it, and gone around the corner to Annette's Petit Veau.

But, short of funds, we didn't and Homer, already sweating from climbing three flights of stairs, said he was used to steaming heat in places like Viet Nam. He then gave another example of his exceptional bravery by stoically coping with the sweat streaming down his face while trying to chew the horrid food I put in front of him. We quite understood when he said he would have to leave early without a cup of coffee because he had to get up early in the morning, or something like that.

When he left, we said our goodbyes and I called out, "Lovely to see you. Come back again."

"W-w-ill do," he said, but he didn't.

I'm in the middle, Ann on the right, Sally behind me and Bridget on the left.
Photograph by: James Fairclough

Pilot Frank, left, another passenger and I survey our crashed Cessna.

The wedding on Virgin Gorda
We triumphantly hoist our "Just Married" banner.
Photograph by: Ray Miles, St. Thomas.

On the beach after the wedding
Tony helps me see the future.
Photograph by: Ray Miles, St. Thomas.

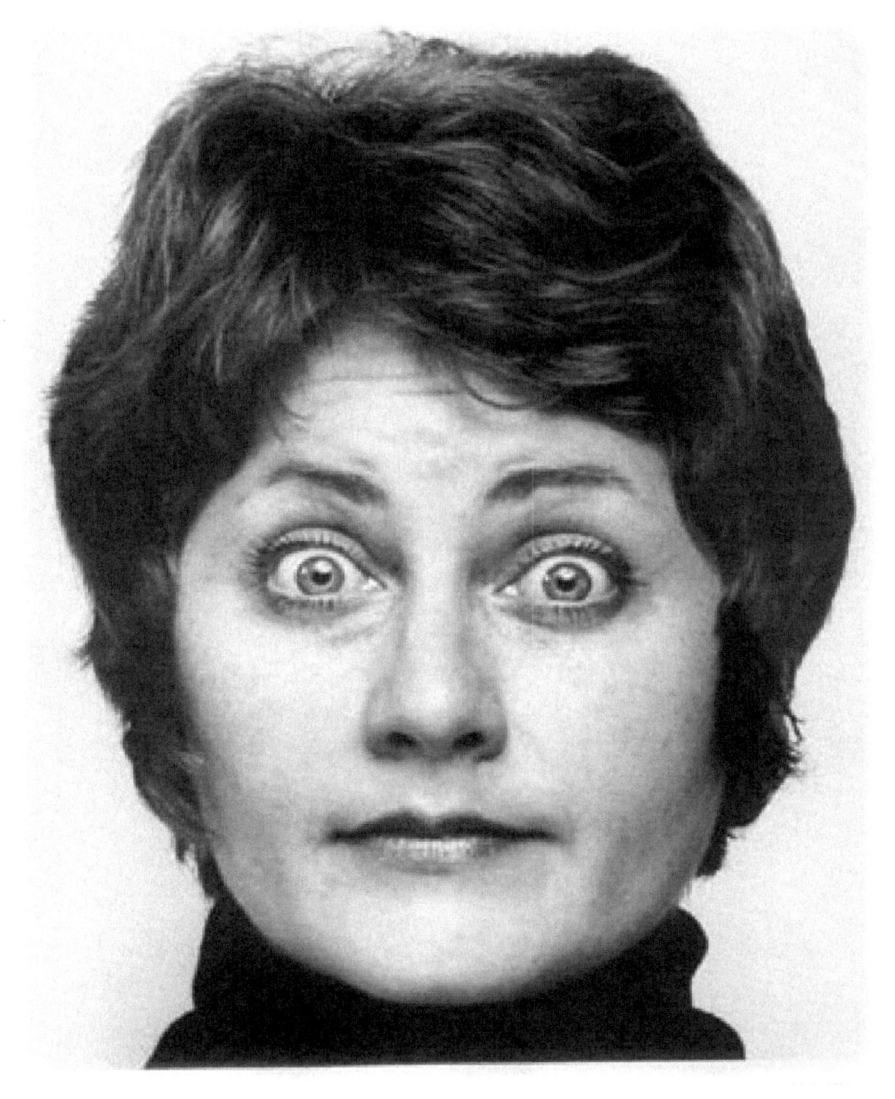

Eyes wide open
I exercise my eyes for and an article in Coronet magazine.
Photograph by: Coronet Magazine

The twins try to look cute
They're identical and I'm not sure which is which
Photograph by: Nikki English, a friend.

The house at Woodstock
Site of hijinks.
Photograph by: Leonora Burton.

Manhattan family scene.
We're on 42nd Street outside the Daily News building.
Photograph by Eddie Kirkman.

Newspaper magnates
Roger and Beth Ailes smile for the camera.
Photograph by: AP Photos.

No friend of Roger
Gordon Stewart conducts the orchestra in a production of the
Beggars Opera at Garrison Landing, NY.
Photograph by: The Paper/Philipstown.info.

CHAPTER EIGHT

Costello's, the scene of the start of the happy hooker's farewell celebration, was a restaurant/bar sited at that time on Third Avenue. It was well-known as a hangout for writers and newspaper hacks but better known for the James Thurber murals on the wall facing the long oaken bar. The cartoonist was said to have drawn pictures of the war between men and women on the wall to pay off his tab during the Depression. On another wall was a bunch of cartoons drawn by artists like Bill Gallo (Basement Bertha} of the Daily News, Tony's newspaper just around the corner, and Stan Lee (Spiderman}. Hanging above a mirror behind the bar was a broken baton, said to have splintered when Ernest Hemingway used it to batter John O'Hara's skull. True? Nobody knows but after a night in Costello's you were inclined to believe anything.

When the tavern moved from Third Avenue to E.44th St., the wall cartoons and Hemingway's broken stick went with it. Costello's also boasted the worst waiter in New York, a title proudly accepted by the recipient, Herbie, a chubby, bespectacled fellow of mittel-European descent whose walking speed was something like .005 m.p.h. He would pad around in his lumpy tuxedo, grubby white apron and lace-less tennis shoes, mumbling incoherently, dropping plates on the tables with little regard for what each diner had ordered. Often he would take the plates of food to the wrong table, muttering angrily as he was redirected. He would ignore calls for ketchup or another beer or, simply, knives and forks. Wiseacres at the bar said he was aiming for the title, worst waiter in the world. They were wise enough never to eat at Costello's, but enjoyed watching unwary diners growing increasingly exasperated as they waited and waited for Herbie to reach their table with their order. When and if it arrived, there was usually a thumb, maybe two, stuck in the gravy. The food was pretty bad, too. Herbie's tips, if any, would be miserly which in a vicious circle made him even more recalcitrant.

Tony and I were there one night waiting for my visiting father to show up before going for dinner at the Oyster Bar at Grand Central. After dad went bankrupt and I was pulled out of my English boarding school, he and mother retreated to a little house in Worthing on the English southeast coast. He wangled a job as an executive with the charity, Help the Aged, which is now called something else, and he was sent around the world on various missions. My lovely, laughter-loving mother fell ill in Worthing. I was at the Frankfurt Book Fair in Germany when I got word that she didn't have much longer. I flew to see her and was at her bedside when she died.

In Costello's, Tony and I talked about dad's new friend. A couple of nights earlier we had dined with him and Ruth, a pleasant widowed New Yorker he had met on a Mediterranean cruise. Mum had died only 13 months earlier. A quick worker, my father. It seemed they were now engaged to marry.

During that dinner, concerned as ever about his diabetes, I asked dad if he had taken his insulin. Ruth looked startled. He hadn't bothered to tell her of his affliction. However, while he was away in the bathroom, she confided that he had told her of his work for the intelligence agency MI6 which was news to me. She was impressed which, I suppose, was my father's intent. My eyebrows shot up but I said nothing.

MI6 was the British nest of spies which conducted espionage abroad. Its cousin was MI5 which handled counter espionage at home and I once had a fleeting contact with it. A girl I knew invited me to share her apartment in London {in Chelsea, not far from George Smiley's home on Bywater St.} and I agreed to move in. She was a secretary at MI5 and she said that because the job involved state secrets I would be investigated but that was a mere formality. It wasn't. My mother telephoned to ask why men were snooping around in Newport asking questions about me.

I explained the situation and all seemed well. But then my flatmate said, "Sorry, Leonora, but you're going to have to move out of the flat. Orders from on high."

It turned out that the snoopers had discovered I had once been a member of a Newport amateur dramatic society. Quite innocent one might have thought, but not so. Unbeknownst to me, some of the eager lovers of drama were also enthusiastic Welsh nationalists. They were suspected by MI5 of trying to blow up dams which had been built in Wales to create reservoirs to supply water to English cities.

The amateur dynamiters objected to the flooding of Welsh valleys for the benefit of the arrogant English. In one case, I later heard, they had bought explosives of dubious effectiveness from the IRA. When the saboteurs tried to set off an explosion at a dam they were rewarded with nothing more than a puff of smoke and the dislodging of a couple of bricks. I had no idea such plots were being cooked up in between rehearsals for plays by Congreve and Noel Coward but my ignorance didn't save me from MI5's suspicions and I had to find another apartment.

In Costello's, the bar's telephone rang—it was always ringing—and I was told it was for me. It was Ruth and she sounded distraught. "You have to come," she said. "It's terrible. Your father's dead."

Ruth gave me her address in Riverdale in the northwest corner of the Bronx, a section that somehow had escaped the fires demolishing the South Bronx. We rushed out, flagged a taxi and gave the driver the address. I clutched Tony's hand as we drove north. No tears, I felt numb. Ruth occupied a spacious apartment on an upper floor of a high-rise. She was in a state of shock but she was not alone. There was a uniformed policeman who had arrived to make sure the body, covered by a sheet and lying on a pull-out bed in the living room, wasn't moved until the medical officer's team had given permission. Also standing around looking uncomfortable was the choir from Ruth's church. They weren't there to sing hymns over dad. It seemed that she had called one member who, in turn, told others and they all came round to show their support. It was like a cocktail party with the guests awkwardly waiting for drinks to be served and the drinks never arriving. Everybody was trying to ignore the body under the sheet. I caught Tony looking amused by the bizarre scene, almost ready to burst out laughing. Idiot. I gave him the Fairclough glare. His expression immediately switched to the correct one, grim and mournful.

Ruth wanted everybody to understand that she and my father had been held up at some event the night before and arrived in Riverdale later than expected. She had invited him to stay with her instead of trying to find a cab and trundling all the way down to his hotel in Manhattan and then returning the next day. She particularly wanted to make it clear that my father had not occupied her bed but had stretched out on the pull-out bed in the living room. She had slept alone in the bedroom.

Ruth had gone to work in the morning, leaving, as she thought, daddy asleep on the pull-out. When she returned home, she at first assumed he was still asleep until she discovered he was lifeless. To me, it was obvious what had happened. He hadn't taken his insulin. He had gone into a coma and he had died. I wondered if he had deliberately invited the coma and death but, of course, we would never know.

Growing more and more uncomfortable, we waited and waited for the medical examiner. Time dragged. Nobody knew what to say. The cop looked as though he would rather be on the street chasing drug dealers and murderers. I still felt numb. It was as though a cog had slipped. There was a touch of the surreal. My father was Newport, belonged in Newport, and here he was suddenly dead in the Bronx in New York, a foreign land. Two days later, at home in Manhattan, I woke up in the middle of the night and slipped into the living room where my father's few personal belongings, his watch, wallet, passport, business cards lay on a table. As I went through them, I finally wept.

In the apartment in Riverdale, waiting, I eventually called my doctor in Manhattan and explained the situation. I had registered my father with him as a diabetic in case anything happened, which it had.

With the medical examiner still not appearing—there must have been a rich harvest of bodies lying around New York City that night—he kindly agreed to drive up and certify the death from diabetes. This he did, and then phoned the M.E.'s office to report that he had signed the death certificate. They agreed to the removal of the body. I called the Frank E. Campbell funeral home in Manhattan and they promised to come up and pick up dad.

Another long wait for the hearse during which the guests, including the cop, drifted away. It was well after midnight when the undertakers arrived. It had been a long night that probably had lasted three or four hours but seemed more like twelve.

In New York, the Frank E. Campbell funeral home is THE place for last rites and an efficient farewell to the loved one. Its customers, if that's the right word, ranged from Jackie Kennedy and Judy Garland to James Cagney and hoodlum Frank Costello. The list of notables dispatched by the funeral home is endless. It's an honor, really, to be buried or cremated by Frank E. Campbell. If you're of any significance in the world, that's the place for you. It seemed only appropriate then that my odd duck of a father should end up there,

A consultation by phone with my sisters brought the decision that he should be cremated in America. Father must have been well thought of by "Help the Aged." They very kindly insisted that they would pay the expenses of the funeral. Just send them the bill. A memorial service would be held later in Wales. So Tony and I went to discuss dad's future movements with the famous undertakers. The first thing we noticed as we sat waiting for attention was a box of tissues within easy reach of any tearful mourner. The tissues were black. "How thoughtful," said Tony. We both managed to keep our expressions appropriately mournful.

A solemn-faced young man appeared and expressed appropriate sympathy for our sad loss. Then we got down to business.

"We have a beautiful casket that might suit you," he said.

"How much?"

"Well, I believe it's about $7,000."

"My father is being cremated," I said.

84

"So I understand."

"So the beautiful casket will be burned with my father."

"Of course."

"I don't think we need such an expensive coffin that's going to be destroyed in a few seconds."

Hell, this was being paid for by a charity in Britain. We didn't want to spend thousands of their dollars that could be used for something far more worthy. We started going down the list of cheaper and cheaper coffins. Finally we arrived at the least expensive of all.

"It's made of cardboard," the counselor said reproachfully.

"We'll take it."

He sighed, made a note and said, "What about the hearse and the limousine? Will there be many guests?"

"No, there won't. What's the least expensive hearse you've got?" He shook his head and gave up. Clearly we weren't what Frank E. Campbell expected of their clients.

"We can let you have a Volkswagen bus," he said sorrowfully.

"We'll take it." And we did, following the miserable hearse to the crematorium in our little car. We didn't uphold the American tradition of funeral parties turning on their headlights. There didn't seem any point. Ruth was there for the brief ceremony, white-faced and somber. It might have been the cheapest funeral in the storied history of Frank E. Campbell and I suspected that if the Frank E. Campbell had a black list of unwelcome corpses we would be on it.

Afterwards, Ruth said she would collect the ashes and we were happy to let her have them. The three of us promised to keep in touch. We never saw her again.

But more than a year later I got a telephone call from Frank E. Campbell. The voice was disapproving.

"Your father's ashes. We still have them. We've had them all this time and they haven't been collected." Goodness, Ruth must have changed her mind or perhaps, in the depth of her grieving, forgotten her promise.

Tony went to the funeral parlor and picked up the little wooden box of ashes. He dug a hole on the hillside of our Woodstock property and buried them. It's a pity that father wasn't around for it all. It was the sort of grisly episode he would have enjoyed no end.

CHAPTER NINE

Often, hidden under my pillow would be a paperback Regency romance. It wasn't exactly a secret, more just private, that I was addicted to these tales of dashing, aristocratic heroes and gorgeous, sometimes fiery, heroines. Part of the books' attraction, I'm sure, was that they presented a world entirely different to modern times, particularly to the noisy hustle of Manhattan. The background was usually the serene landscape of England. Pure escapism. One of my favorite writers was the prolific but under-rated Georgette Heyer, probably under-rated because she was so prolific. I would read them and, probably like hundreds of other readers, say to myself, "I could write this stuff." I knew all the Regency period words and phrases like "the ton"—the sophisticated nobility and upper class—and "the fichu"—a piece of silk to hide the chest of modest ladies—and "I'm in dun territory"—I'm broke, dude.

Suddenly I had the time to find out if I really could write this stuff. To accommodate the twins we had moved to a two-bedroom, doorman apartment on 58th St., seductively close to Bloomingdales. Here, every afternoon, I would put the little monsters down for their two-hour nap, pick up my pencil and start scribbling. My dedication to the Regency period led me to find time to take fencing lessons so that I could write knowledgably about duels between the noble hero and the sinister villain. I had scores of plots in my head and although I wasn't fit to touch the floor-sweeping hem of Jane Austen's gown, hell, as she would never say, who was? Never mind, I was enjoying myself. The first one was called "Lady Tara" and I sold it to Fawcett Crest. One unit of Fawcett was bought around that time by, who else? the voracious Warner Communications. Dedicated to "My mother and friend," the "Lady Tara" book jacket promised readers "A spirited novel of love, adventure and a young beauty's dangerous deception." What fun. How could a Regency romance fan resist? I was off to the races. Titles were no problem. I simply slapped the first name of the heroine on to the cover.

More books followed, one after another, and they seemed to find a readership. By the time I called a halt I had produced more than a dozen romances, some of them written for a complicated reason for the German market. The only sour note was struck by one male reader who objected when I wrote about the hero of one book who "under his tight britches felt a stirring in his loins"—or something like that.—when he glimpsed the heroine in dishabille. Indignantly, my correspondent wrote that he didn't expect to find that sort of language in a Regency romance. It was quite disgusting, he declared. So sorry I disturbed the purity of your thoughts, I didn't reply. Well, I didn't realize I was writing for prudish men. I had to admit, though, that Jane would undoubtedly have agreed with him.

I didn't venture into the realm of stirring loins again although later writers offered much more salaciously descriptive tales and did very well out of them, thank you. By then, my indignant letter writer surely had given up and switched to Tom Clancy.

Tony, meanwhile, was contemplating his third book. His first, a non-fiction account of an undercover detective's adventures in the New York drug world, joined the best-seller list in Newsday, the Long Island daily, but he suspected that was because so many cops lived out on the island. His second, a World War 11 novel involving the IRA's cooperation with the Nazis was edited by Ned Chase, the father of comedian/actor Chevy Chase. Ned Chase, who seemed to admire the title, The Coventry Option, more than the actual book, complained that editors no longer edited. Instead, they spent all their time acquiring books. And that was years ago. The book got good reviews but didn't bust any blocks, perhaps, Tony reflected, because Irish-American readers who sympathized with the IRA didn't fancy it. Hah!

While reporting for the Daily News he had come across the story of Roy Shuster, a convict who had struggled for years to win release from Clinton prison upstate in Dannemora and finally, on the orders of a federal judge outraged at his treatment, walked free.

Shuster, an accomplished tap dancer in the 20s, had shot and killed his wife during a bitter divorce battle. He said he had meant to kill her lawyer, a plan which if successful might have drawn more sympathy from a jury. In Dannemora, he was dubbed a trouble-maker and the guards had an answer to that. Like others before him, he was declared insane by a compliant doctor and moved to a lunatic asylum next door to the prison There he was held for decades, much longer than his sentence called for, because of course he was criminally insane and couldn't be released to become a danger to the public. What a country.

Shuster became something of a prison lawyer and, over the years, managed to take his case to federal court in Manhattan. There, the chief appeals judge, after considering Shuster's evidence, ordered his immediate release and the closing of the asylum. This judge, Irving Kaufman, had sentenced the atom spies, Ethel and Julius Rosenberg, to death in the 1950s. Announcing his decision, Kaufman said, "Although we are reasonably certain that the shocking story revealed in The Gulag Archipelago could not take place in this country, the facts of Roy Shuster's case are reminiscent of Solzhenitsyn's treatise . . . We can no longer sit by and permit the state to continue toying with his freedom."

Tony thought there might be a book in it and began interviewing Shuster and doing research. I met Shuster when Tony decided it would be a good idea to take him to the quiet peace of Woodstock where they could talk uninterrupted. On the drive up, I sat next to Tony who was driving while Shuster, an inoffensive-looking little chap, sat in the back. On the Palisades Parkway, Tony noted that the gas gauge was hovering over empty but certainly there was enough to get us to the gas station up the road. There wasn't. Idiot. Tony pulled over, took a can from the trunk and set off walking to the gas station

"Be right back," he shouted. I was left with Shuster.

Suddenly I realized I was alone in the dark with a murderer. All he had to do was reach over the back of my seat, strangle me, toss out my body and take off in the car. Perhaps he wouldn't bother to toss me out. He might just leave my corpse in the passenger seat, bury me later. My imagination had gone antic. Cool it, Leonora, he can't take off in the car because there's no gas. No, but he could take off on foot, leaving me completely deceased. I twisted around to look over my shoulder. Shuster was sitting peacefully, occasionally commenting on the different world he was encountering after his release. Sure, just lulling me into a sense of security. I put my fingers on the door handle so that I could jump out if he made a sudden move. Maybe a parkway cop would stop to see why we were sitting there at the side of the road. Oooh, please.

No cop turned up but after about 24-hours—all right, it just seemed like that—Tony returned with a can of fuel. I didn't say anything. It would have been exceedingly bad manners to complain to Tony that he had left me alone with a murderer while said murderer was sitting immediately behind us listening to the discussion. After we arrived in Woodstock and Shuster had gone to bed, Tony and I had a full and frank chat.

As it turned out, Tony abandoned the project on the grounds that it was difficult, if not impossible, to make an interesting story out of Shuster being locked up for years. Roy had some good stories like living in a cell next to the one occupied by mobster Lucky Luciano. Shuster said he caught a squirrel and made a pet of it. Luciano decided he wanted the squirrel, so he took it. When Roy complained at the larceny, Luciano, who pretty well owned the prison, gave him a look that sent him stumbling off in a cloud of apologies. But for us there was a sequel of sorts. Through contacts at the Daily News, we were able to arrange for Shuster to occupy a nice, government-subsidized apartment available to aging show business folk on W42nd St. His claim rested on his early career as a tap dancer, not on his later career as a killer and convict.

After his death, a couple arrived in New York from the Mid West, found us and announced they were Shuster's only living relatives and therefore his heirs. They had heard that a book was being written, or had been published, about Roy Shuster. They danced around the reason for their visit but it soon became clear they were interested in any financial rewards that might be accruing to his estate. Just interested, they said. Told the book had never been written, never would be, they looked at us suspiciously but finally they went unhappily away. They had come from Wisconsin or somewhere like that to the wicked city in search of a pot of gold and left without even a thimble full.

What they didn't know, and we didn't know at that time, was that in a later novel, entirely fiction, Tony would use as a subsidiary character a jail bird who was transferred from his cell to a lunatic asylum because he was troublesome.

Chapter Ten

An ex-pat friend of ours once said, "If you stay here in the States for five years, you won't go back home. You'll stay permanently." Perhaps she was right but although I had been in New York for more than five years my bonds with the U.K., particularly with Wales, were still strong. A couple of months after the birth of the twins, we took them back to be christened to a little church near the home of my sister, Sally, in Wales. A party with all our relatives followed.

"When are you coming back to the U.K.?" they asked. I didn't know.

Tony had a job he enjoyed. I was happy for the time being in New York, had developed a circle of good friends, was having fun and I had learned that by no means were all Americans rude, grasping and immature. The ones I was close to, like Nestor Bryant, were kind, generous, loved to laugh and were not overbearingly full of themselves. And as the children grew up, they would grow up American, with American accents and American attitudes.

A few years later, David English, the Daily Mail editor in London, called Tony and invited him to fly to London and work for a couple of months at the Mail. David's idea was that Tony could file stories about the U.K. for the NY Daily News when not writing for the Mail. The notion was entirely possible because Tony, under the union contract, was owed a lot of time by the News for all the weeks he had spent on the road covering news stories. The deal was made, although the Daily News was not interested in free stories from London. Silly lot. We realized later that David had more in mind.

I wasn't going to miss this opportunity for a return to Wales, even if it was only for a short time. Sally and John, her husband, agreed to play hosts to me and the children while Tony was accommodated in a tiny apartment just off Fleet Street, a three-minute walk to the Mail. Financially it was a plus because London reporters had a system of large expense accounts—"Of course I had to hire three camels and two interpreters because it was the only way to get across the desert for the story." Tony was living on his expenses and banking his generous salary.

There was more than one benefit. The twins, now aged about three, had developed their own language which was indecipherable to anybody else. Little beasts. They could talk away and we didn't know what the hell they were saying. The answer lay with Sally's four children, all older than our two and therefore, of course, much admired by the twins. Sally's kids went to work and trained Robert and David to speak a civilized language that everybody else could understand. What a relief to discover they hadn't been plotting to do terrible things to mummy because she had been making them go to bed when they didn't want to.

At the end of the two months in the U.K., David English took Tony to lunch at a very expensive West End restaurant and offered him a permanent job as a reporter on the Daily Mail. It would mean moving to London. The money would be very good, better than he was getting in New York. Unlike the Daily News in New York which was drifting downward, the Mail, under English, had become highly successful, its circulation and advertising on the rise, so money was flowing freely. English's philosophy was that the heart and soul of journalism was the news gathering operation and that those responsible for it should be well rewarded. To hell with the number crunchers. Although Tony admired David English enormously, as the most talented pop journalist of his time. there were problems. Among them, David liked to set up creative tension. Sometimes he would order two reporters to take the same assignment to see who would produce the best story, something no editor in the States would do because they took their work far too seriously to play games like that, perhaps too seriously. That sort of thing created competition but also dissension among the reporting staff. Who was the best? On Fleet Street there was a ruthlessness that disturbed Tony.

Tony and David had known each other since their early 20s when they had shared an apartment in south London with two other reporters, one of them a brilliant razzle-dazzle pianist. David decreed that they must hold a big party and that Des, the pianist, must play for the guests. They had no piano so they rented one and then found it wouldn't go up the stairs. David reacted by renting a driver and his crane which picked up the piano and lifted it so that it could pass through a big window upstairs. Whatever David wants David gets. He had also pinned up a notice backstage at the Adelphi Theater on the Strand inviting members of the Tiller Girls dancing troupe performing there to attend the bash. A dozen pretty young things poured in and David later married one of them.

At one point, David and Tony freelanced together, unsuccessfully. David burned with ambition to become the first Fleet Street editor under the age of 40 and achieved that historic height although some skeptics suggested that he had forgotten a year or two of his life to satisfy his ambition.

Charm, he was loaded to the brim with it. A number of times I watched his technique. When he was introduced to a new acquaintance, his boyish face beamed, his hand shot out to draw the person to him while he launched into a series of questions with enormous interest in the answers as if this was the most fascinating person he had ever come across. His concentration was total. The thing was, he was genuinely curious about other people, whether they were the cleaning woman or a member of royalty. You couldn't fake it and I could see people just warming to him as they talked. They knew they were pretty damned interesting and here was David soaking it all up. He had them and he knew it.

When the twins arrived he attended their christening in Wales and became godfather to one of them. He made frequent visits to New York because he was fascinated by America, its exuberance, drive and power. Much later, when he became chairman of his newspaper group, he had dealings with business executives on both sides of the Atlantic. I asked him once which executives, British or American, were the smartest. Without hesitation he said, "Oh, the Americans, no doubt about it." David really liked Americans.

One of his favorite photographs was of him talking to Lyndon Johnson in the White House. Because the picture was taken from a very low angle you could see a concealed microphone sticking out from the arm of the President's chair. David used to say that if anything new and interesting emerged in the U.K. it had been in the U.S. 10 years before. On his visits to New York, he would shower presents on the children. It was fun to match wits with him but he usually won, at least he claimed he had. Some Americans have a rule: no discussion of politics or religion at the dinner table. David's view was the reverse: if there hadn't been a loud argument then the dinner party was a failure. He liked to play Speaker of the House, calling on this guest or that to offer evidence to buttress their arguments. At the end of the debate he would declare the winner which of course started up the argument again.

As the children grew up we followed David's dinner table philosophy and encouraged them to argue about anything at all, including religion and politics. Sometimes their discussions would grow so heated that one of them would storm away from the table which was taken as signaling defeat in the battle of words.

David could be brutal. Once while Tony was in London David invited him to attend an editorial conference at the Mail, perhaps to demonstrate his omnipotence. David presided benevolently over the discussion of news stories and at the end the lower level editors withdrew. In came Sue, the features editor and a very good one. There were just the three of them. She was extremely attractive and she wore an extreme mini skirt. David then set about eviscerating her. Every feature story she pitched to him he rejected with cutting scorn. Sue was tough enough to endure it without breaking down but it must have been hell for her, especially in front of Tony.

Tony told me about the episode and I asked if he had questioned David afterward about his behavior. Shouldn't Tony have expressed his discomfort? He shook his head. "David," he said, "could be a bit of a prude and perhaps he was offended by the tiny mini skirt although I enjoyed it.

Perhaps there was another reason entirely. Perhaps he was showing off for my benefit. I should have asked him about it but didn't. He was the editor and editors were potentates on Fleet Street who could do whatever the hell they liked."

As for the invitation to join the Daily Mail, Tony told David he would have to think about it which meant he would have to discuss it with me. I was undecided.

One reason for my questioning the appeal of America was the ERA, the Equal Rights Amendment. No, I wasn't a feminist but what sort of country could reject a law that simply said men and women should be treated equally? I had done some shallow research and found it was almost impossible to amend the constitution significantly in modern times because amendments had to be accepted by Congress and ratified by three-fourths of the states. Only 27 amendments had passed and 10 of those comprised the Bill of Rights. It was that darned Constitution again, the one that was amended around 1920 finally to allow women to vote. How kind. The ERA was blocked and now lies gathering dust somewhere in the congressional archives.

Tony and I talked over what we should do and it went something like this:

"The weather," he said.

"The weather?" I asked.

"Winter in New York, crisp, glistening snow, skating at Rockefeller Center, skiing in Vermont, warm houses wherever you go."

"Yes, but . . ."

"Winter in London, raw, wet, cold, miserable for six months with unheated houses and everybody, including us, sniffling with colds." I couldn't help remembering so many summers in Wales when my father had driven the family to the beach and we had sat in the car staring dolefully at the gray waves while the rain hammered down on the roof. Then, after our day out, we went home.

"Spring in St. James Park," I said.

"Spring in Central Park."

"Pubs," I said. "Lovely pubs. And they have the death penalty in America."

"What, you're planning to whack me?" he inquired. "The English class system. It stinks."

"David English says it's disappearing," I muttered.

"It's not."

"In America, the system of government is crazy." I had him there.

"That's one reason news stories are so great over there," he said. "That's why I love it. There's always something ridiculous happening. Guns, crime, political corruption, riots, death row, executions, religious nuts, crazy trials. Marvellous."

I knew which way this was going. Tony preferred America. I was 50-50. It would be nice to say I believed that if he would be happier there then I would be happy as well. If he was happy, I was happy. When I expressed this thought to Tony he nodded and smirked insufferably.

Closer to the truth was my distaste at the thought of all the complications of selling our Woodstock house, collecting all our belongings, including the twins, and shipping all of us to the U.K., finding somewhere to live over there, readjusting. And suppose we discovered that we had made a terrible mistake, yearning for the good things, and there were some, in America while grumbling about the weather and the bad things, and there were some, in the U.K.

Case closed. We packed, grabbed the kids and headed for the airport.

*   *   *

To me, the most irritating thing about Americans was that they knew almost nothing about Wales if they knew anything at all. Hearing the word, Wales, they would go on about "That wonderful book about a whale, Moby Dick" or say "That's in England, isn't it?" Too many didn't know it was the most beautiful country in the world inhabited by the finest human beings. They didn't know it produced the best singers (see Charlotte Church and Katherine Jenkins), the most gorgeous women (see Catherine Zeta Jones), the most handsome men (see Richard Burton—real name, Jenkins), the most stirring orators (See David Lloyd George and Aneurin Bevan) and, of more importance, the greatest rugby players on earth. So annoying.

They didn't know that Wales had been oppressed for centuries by England which was determined to expunge Welsh from the world's languages. Typical English arrogance. At one point, Welsh children were punished for speaking in their native tongue. Any child who spoke Welsh in class would have a block of wood called "the not" hung around their necks until they could pass it to another pupil caught speaking Welsh. At the end of the class, the child with "the not" around his or her neck would be beaten. But the courageous Welsh won in the end. Today, teaching of the Welsh language is compulsory in all schools in Wales.

Probably the best way to describe Welsh attitudes towards the Irish would be that they were as neutral as Dublin was during the war. My view was more complicated. During the war, Ireland had remained aloof like Sweden and Switzerland while a monster roamed Europe slaughtering millions. Further, I was dismayed when I read that the prim-mouthed Irish president, Eamon de Valera, on Adolf Hitler's suicide in 1945, had paid a visit to the German Minister in Dublin to offer his condolences and then signed the condolence book De Valera explained to his own satisfaction if nobody else's that it would have been "an act of unpardonable discourtesy to the German nation" not to have expressed his sympathy for their loss. It occurred to me that the German nation had committed numerous acts of unpardonable discourtesy during the war.

Beyond that, thousands of Irish soldiers who had left the military of their homeland to fight with the Allies against Hitler and his war machine were court martialed in Ireland in their absence for desertion. Many were not affected because they had lost their lives on foreign battlefields. Those who survived were punished for their idealism by being put on a black list which meant they lost their pension rights and could take no government jobs. Some became destitute and their children were taken "into care."

Still, both Wales and Ireland had suffered under the English boot. Hundreds of Irish had immigrated to America to escape the disastrous potato famine that England had done little to relieve. The true nobility of the Irish lay with the hundreds of thousands of civilian Irish men and women who turned their backs on their slumbering nation and went off to join the Scots, the Welsh and the English in the forces of the U.S., Canada and Britain struggling with Hitler and his murderous hordes. They helped make sure that Hitler could never strut into Ireland where the Nazis would have made the previous English overlords look like nannies.

Unlike the Irish, the Welsh had finally subscribed to the saying, "If you can't beat them, join them." As a result, Wales sent representatives to Westminster where Lloyd George became the silver-tongued prime minister and Aneurin Bevan, from the South Wales mining valleys, led the successful fight after the war to install a national health service.

One of my few contacts with the Irish developed at school where an Irish girl, Florence McGowan, believed I had said something derogatory about her country. Silly me. She chased me with an Irish shillelagh she had brought to school to show around until I took refuge in the lavatory and locked the door. Afterwards we laughed about it and became good friends.

But the terrorists of the IRA were another matter entirely. Demonstrating was fine. Killing people, including the innocent, was not. In America, I was irritated by the mindless support that Irish-Americans and some newspapers gave to the killers. Certainly, on Bloody Sunday, British paratroopers had shamefully shot and killed peaceful demonstrators and then the London government had white-washed the affair in a bogus investigation. It was a stupid, unforgivable mistake which gave the IRA the excuse they needed to introduce a policy of killing. But the string of murders that the IRA launched for years afterwards, turning my stomach, achieved nothing. Professional Irishmen in New York, the Breslins and the Dalys made heroes out of the "hard men" as they liked to call the IRA gunmen and bombers. Even as the IRA's campaign neared its end with the Good Friday agreement, a splinter group calling itself the Real IRA exploded a bomb in Armagh which killed 29, including 6 children. The IRA condemned it which was nice.

At the height of the Troubles, David English came to New York and invited us to dinner at Frankie and Johnny's steakhouse on Third Avenue in the East 40s. That morning, the Daily News had splashed a story by one of its columnists about Northern Ireland, largely built around an interview he claimed to have had with a British soldier named Christopher Spell. This soldier had talked remarkably frankly about his view of the conflict. He came from a poverty-stricken neighborhood of Birmingham, he said, and he described how, envious of people with money, he sometimes walked from his seedy home to the wealthy suburbs where he would watch the affluent people have a good time drinking.

"What have they got I haven't got?" he asked his mother.

"Everything," she said.

Gunner Spell told stories of firing plastic bullets at Irish children and of officers calling the Irish sub human and Zulus. The soldier said he couldn't understand why he, a youngster from the back streets of Birmingham, was fighting penniless young men like himself who were struggling for their freedom. The detail was remarkable, quite a scoop, including a description of the scene inside the armored car as it roared down the Falls Road with stones and bottles flung against the steel sides.

The article ended, "Spell moved up the street, fired again and the kid from the poor neighborhood of Birmingham continued his war with the poor of Belfast."

David had not seen the article.

"There's something fishy about that story," Tony said. "First, an American journalist would never be allowed to ride in an armored car in the middle of the fighting. Ordinary soldiers never go out on their own or make themselves available to an unknown man who says he's a visiting reporter. There's always the fear of kidnapping. How did the reporter get hold of him? I've been over there and you would never find a despised British soldier wandering around Belfast on his own, a perfect target for the gunmen."

"Second, it's too slick. He's saying what the IRA is saying."

"Third, I worked in Birmingham for a while and know it would take hours to walk out from the inner city to the wealthier suburbs. And he goes out there just to peer through windows at people drinking? It doesn't make sense."

David called the waiter and asked if they had a Daily News lying around. They did and he studied it before standing up and going to the phone. It was around 2 a.m. in London but the night shift was on duty and he ordered them to get to work. When the editor calls at 2 a.m. or 2 p.m. everybody jumps.

The next morning it all began to come together. In London, the Ministry of Defense said they had checked and there was no soldier named Christopher Spell serving anywhere in the British army. There were no soldiers from Birmingham in Belfast. Reporters in New York and London did more digging. With all the evidence in hand, David ordered a two page splash in the Daily Mail, accusing the columnist and the News of publishing a "pack of lies." Under the flaring headline, "The propaganda that inflames America", the articles picked apart the columnist's story paragraph by paragraph until it lay in ruins. David was not averse to assaulting an American newspaper. Some years before, the Washington Post had run an expose of the Daily Mail's Washington correspondent showing that he had invented story after story. The correspondent, who liked to play the professional Englishman in the capital, parading around in a bowler hat, was dubbed "The Faker of Fleet Street." He was fired immediately but the Mail was deeply embarrassed.

Now, Tony found himself in an odd position. On the one hand he worked for the Daily News and owed it his loyalty. When he remarked on the unlikeliness of the story from Belfast he had no idea that it was going to light a trail of gunpowder. It was just conversation until David's instinct for news led him to alert the Mail. Still the truth was the truth. Before the Mail published its expose, Tony passed word to the Daily News editors that they should brace themselves for a storm. Through contacts, he said, he knew that the Daily Mail in London was about to attack the column as false, along with the paper that had published it.

As a result, the editors ordered the columnist in Belfast to fly back to New York immediately. Two of the top editors went out to JFK to meet him. What passed between them is not known but the columnist resigned. He said he stood by his story but was resigning to "save the paper from embarrassment." If he stood by his story, I thought, why didn't he stay and fight? Clearly "a pack of lies" summed it up but it was so inflammatory that it would have brought a rush of cash to the bottles on the bars in New York's Irish pubs collecting for the "boyos" in Belfast.

Tony said the columnist's remarkably foolish mistake was giving a name to his soldier informant. If he had told the same story but used an anonymous soldier he might not have been exposed as a blatant propagandist for the IRA.

In London, Prime Minister Margaret, who had ordered a heavy-handed response to IRA outrages, was delighted. David had given a bloody nose to the IRA and to the professional Irishmen of the New York papers and their followers. Three years later, the IRA tried to assassinate Thatcher by exploding a bomb in the hotel in Brighton where she was staying during the Conservative Party's annual conference. Five innocent people died but not the prime minister. Later, David was awarded a knighthood. Also, after enough time had passed, the columnist was re-hired by the News.

CHAPTER ELEVEN

A truth universally acknowledged is that the East Side of Manhattan was, and is, the home of the most affluent and powerful people in the city, perhaps the country, perhaps the world. Naturally, living among them on the East Side, I often mixed with them. Well, more realistically I should say that I had contact with them.

Our modest 51ˢᵗ Street third storey one bedroom walk-up, so good for exercising the legs, was a few buildings up from a pretty townhouse occupied by a wealthy couple and their young son who was about the same age as the twins. The father was so rich and such a music-lover that every so often he would rent an auditorium at Carnegie Hall, gather a symphony orchestra together and, acting as conductor, give a concert for his relatives, friends and associates, free of charge, one assumes. My contact with them came about because of the twins who turned out to be something of an Open Sesame to the world of the wealthy.

The wife of the amateur symphony orchestra conductor sent her son—call him Michael—to the United Nations nursery school, as did I, and we met while waiting to pick up the kids after school. There was a connection there with the Brits. On the wall of the school's brick building at the intersection of 51st St., and First Avenue was a plaque supposedly marking the site of the hanging by the British during the American revolution of the spy, Nathan Hale. Before he swung, he declared, "I only regret that I have but one life to give for my country." Or so the legend goes. It's believed he was questioned by the British General William Howe near that site but there is disagreement among historians as to the place where the gallows stood.

Waiting outside the school, Michael's mother and I became friendly as we chatted about the problems of raising the little horrors. After we had moved to a larger apartment with two bedrooms to give the twins some space. I would take them to a nearby park where mothers, or more likely nannies, from the neighborhood of multi-millionaires wheeled their kids for an airing. There, the youngsters would play and the mothers and nannies would sit on the benches and chat. There I again came across the wife of the amateur conductor. One day she asked if the next day I would act as nanny and take her Michael to the park with the twins because she was otherwise engaged, an urgent foray to Tiffany's or Lord and Taylor, perhaps.

Sure, said Nanny Leonora. The three boys played well together and one more to watch would be no burden. Off we went to the tiny park, barely wider than the distance you could throw a three-year-old, which overlooked the East River at the end of 57th St.

In its turn, the park was overlooked by the handsome brick townhouse of the secretary-general of the United Nations, whoever he might be. In the middle, inexplicably, stood a weather-worn sculpture of a wild boar, together with a sand-pit.

Some children were not allowed to play in the sand-pit on the grounds that it was loaded with germs and, possibly, dog droppings. I noticed that these kids were often sick. My theory was that they were so cosseted and protected that they never built up immunities.

The gossip on the benches could be delicious. One story passed around was that the parents of a youngster noticed that when he spoke he automatically put his thumb to his ear and his little finger to his mouth as if talking on the phone. Puzzled, the parents set up a hidden camera to watch the nanny who spent more time with the child than they did. The puzzle was solved when they saw that as soon as she was alone with the little boy the nanny picked up the phone presumably to chat with her friends. She spent the whole day with the phone to her ear, hardly ever putting it down. To accomplish this, she did everything around the apartment one-handed. The child, obviously, was aping her style.

The talkative nanny was dismissed and, one hopes, eventually the boy learned to speak without holding his hand up to his ear. Such was life in America among the rich and powerful.

Now, with three children to watch, I stood at the bottom of the walkway down to the park so that none of them could escape. Everything was fine until a squabble broke out between two little girls who looked as though they were about to scratch each other's eyes out. I went over to help sort it out. It took no more than three or four minutes during which, out of the corner of my eye, I noted a woman carrying a child up the walkway.

When I returned to my trio of toddlers, one thing immediately became clear. There were only two of them. Michael, the child I was supposed to be nannying, had vanished.

To say I panicked is an understatement. At that time, New York was engulfed in crime. He had been seized by a child molester! He had been carried off to be held for a huge ransom! A mass murderer had chosen his latest little victim!

I was numb with fear. Call the police? I could see the headlines when the little boy's body was found: Nanny Lets Killer Grab Baby of Rich Family.

As I looked frantically around the park for the missing toddler, I noticed movement at the top of the walk-way. It was the only way out of the park. I raced up and found Michael being installed by a woman in the back of a black limousine with a chauffeur at the wheel.

"What the hell is going on?" I demanded, and ran to stand in front of the car in case the chauffeur decided to take off. "Stay where you are," I shouted at the driver. He shrugged and turned off the engine. I went to confront the woman.

"Look," she said, "I'm the housekeeper. We were sent to pick up Michael and take him home and that's what we're doing." I looked at Michael, a bright kid, and he nodded. "She's Rose," he said.

My overwhelming relief turned into cold fury. "They didn't tell you Michael was with me? That you had to contact me before you ran off with him?"

"They just said, Pick up Michael from the park and that's what we did"

The anger was still with me when I telephoned Michael's house and eventually reached his mother. I let my emotions spill out until I had nothing more to say. It was a pretty good tantrum, the sort of furious outburst that I doubt she had heard since childhood, if then.

"I'm sorry you feel that way," she said coldly and put down the phone. I never talked to her again.

My only other experience with a black limousine in Manhattan developed when Robert and David were born. Tony and I emerged from the front entrance of the hospital, Beth Israel, each with one babe in arms, to find expats Philip Finn and wife, Anne-Marie, waiting for us. They lived in the apartment immediately below ours and had come to make sure we got home safely. With them was a chauffeured limosine which they had kindly hired for the occasion. Thus, the twins started life in the lap of donated luxury. Hah. They would soon have to get used to hard rations.

I don't know if our good friend, the much-loved Brigga, was wealthy although she had a splendid townhouse in the most fashionable section of Greenwich Village. Much as one might like to, you couldn't go around saying, "Are you rich?" and "How much money have you got?"

Brigga had the ravishing looks of a top model, plus warmth that I doubt is to be found on the runways. We met at a party and, taking to each other, became good friends. It was a comfortable relationship. We would go down to the Village and have drinks and dinner in her little backyard. Occasionally, she would come up to Woodstock for a day or two. It was one of the happiest periods of my American life. I had a husband, children, good friends, American and expats, and was now really at home to New York I enjoyed the good things there and laughed at the bad.

One evening, Tony and I went down to dinner at the Greenwich Village house. There were other guests and when we walked in, one of them looked up at me, then suddenly told Brigga he had to go. Astonished, she showed him out before coming back and saying, "That was strange. I wonder what it was all about."

"I can tell you," I said and then launched into the story. The man was a doctor and he had been my gynecologist. He had been recommended to me because I had had some miscarriages. Supposedly he was the one who could diagnose my problem. He had no answers, but suggested that it might help if I lost a few pounds. He gave me a prescription for some pills which I took to my local pharmacist, a friendly character with whom I had occasionally chatted. The pharmacist looked surprised and disapproving when he saw the prescription.

"D'you know what these are?" he said.

"To help me lose weight."

"They're speed," he said. "I'll give you one but that's it." Speed was methamphetamine, an addictive drug, I later learned, that made you hyper active. Withdrawal effects included mental depression and increased appetite which hardly seemed a good way to lose weight.

I was furious and so was Tony. I telephoned the doctor and gave him a dose of the Fairclough rant. This was the doctor who had retreated so hurriedly from Brigga's dinner table when he saw me, the harridan.

Following the speed episode, I turned for help to my lovely, trusted, regular physician who had helped me with my father's death certificate. He put me in touch with another gynecologist that he guaranteed would not play games with prescriptions.

When I was pregnant, my new gynecologist recommended that, because of previous medical problems and because twins were on the way,

I should have a Caesarian or, easier to spell, a C-section when the moment arrived. That's not the way it happened.

I felt the first labor pains while at home on 58th St. I called Tony at his office but he was out on a story. I called the doctor. He said it was probably false labor pains but I should go to Beth Israel hospital downtown because he was about to go there. I took a cab.

When I arrived, I was rushed into surgery. The little monsters were on their way. My physician had been held up in traffic so a young substitute was assigned to me. He struck me as cold and insensitive with no sense of humor. He said there was no time for a C-section; I would have to do it the old fashioned way. The midwife was very different, sympathetic and understanding. She held my hand during the two hours of labor. After Robert emerged, cheery Leonora said, "Who wants to bet the next one will be a girl?" The doctor was not amused. The midwife giggled and said, "No betting in surgery. Just get on with it." David arrived five minutes after Robert.

That's how things went as the boys grew up. Robert would struggle to crawl, to use his hands, to walk. David would closely watch his brother's pioneering efforts at crawling and walking until Robert had succeeded. Then, having studied the technique, David would do the same much more easily because he had seen how to manage it. In his teen years, David developed the celebrated icy, blue-eyed glare of the Faircloughs.

Brigga loved to laugh but there was a sadness lurking behind her smiling eyes. Her husband had died not long before and she was left with their three children, although two of them were approaching adulthood and the oldest was in her 20s. The second-born, Natasha, became a criminal defense lawyer who could be seen often on TV analyzing cases of interest to the public.

When we met her, Brigga was putting the finishing touches to an enormous volume about pre-Columbian South American artifacts written by her late husband, Alan, together with brilliant pictures.

After the twins arrived, she agreed to be godmother to Robert. And she had a suggestion. Why didn't we take a break from the babies and fly off on a vacation? She would love to look after them in our absence. For our part, we knew nobody we would trust more with the babes and we agreed it was a brilliant idea. Off we went to, where else? St. Thomas to visit Ray Miles and the Lord Nelson and the church on Virgin Gorda where we had married.

As the boys grew up, Brigga came to love them as if they were her own, now three adults. She spoiled them and read to them and played with them.

Brigga had a number of admirers but the most intense pursuit was launched by a young Australian journo (Aussi for newspaper hack) named Don Willisee who came from a well-known family of politicians and media stars. His father had been a minister in the Australian government. Don wanted to take Brigga to Western Australia to meet his family and to see if she liked the country enough to move there with him. She agreed and off they went.

The next we heard of Brigga was shattering. She had died in a horrible road accident. The report we got was that she had driven off alone to spend some time on a beach, perhaps to consider her future. After leaving the beach she was motoring home when she drove into a head-on collision with a truck, dying instantly. Nobody knew why she was driving on the wrong side of the road but the likeliest reason seemed to be that she had forgotten Australians drive on the left. Disoriented, she might have forgotten she was no longer in the States. Once, in Woodstock, we had picked up our car after a service and Tony had blithely steered the car into the left hand lane as if he were in the U.K. I screamed at him and he just managed to get out of the way of oncoming traffic. Phew.

There was a memorial service for Brigga in New York and afterwards we lunched with her children in the Village but it was a sad and awkward gathering. With Brigga gone, we didn't see much more of them.

Chapter Twelve

After Tony's father died, his mother found herself living alone in a cottage in Oxfordshire. She had never learned to drive a car and so, in her 80s, she was more or less trapped out of walking distance from the few shops in the closest village. She struggled to cope but it was an impossible situation. She floated the suggestion of joining us in America and we quickly agreed. The house in Woodstock would have been perfect but it was too distant from New York for Tony to commute every day. We started looking. One possibility was a pleasant apartment in Tudor City, a complex at the eastern end of 42nd St. It included a maid's room which she could have used as her own. But there were problems. The room was small and the idea of an old lady from the heart of the Oxfordshire countryside being pitched into the horn-honking, siren-shrieking streets of midtown Manhattan was daunting.

Searching the advertisements in the New York Times, I found a house within our means in a village called Cold Spring. Looking at a map, I found it was 50 miles north of Manhattan but, further investigation showed, it was on the Metro North line with fast trains so that Tony could reach Grand Central and his office in little more than an hour. Also, if while at home, he was dispatched out of town there was an airport only half-an-hour away, much easier than flogging out to LaGuardia or JFK. We went up to examine the house which was just around the corner from Main Street. It was, in fact, two cottages that had been joined to make one house. It had two of everything . . . . Two fireplaces, two staircases, two bathrooms. Immediately across the road from the house was a wooded hill.

Later we learned it was known locally as Hash Hill. It was highly popular among teenagers from the high school who got up to who-knows-what, although the title offered a clue.

The house needed work but we fell in love with it. To consummate that love, we had to sell, oh dear, Woodstock with all its memories. So long, Woodstock and Nestor Bryant, it was wonderful to know you but we've found a new sweetheart. Still, I was reminded of Nestor every day by a couch on which he had been inclined to fall asleep after a Woodstock dinner. We dubbed it the Nestor Memorial Couch. We still have it today.

It was a wrench but we bought the Cold Spring house and immediately found that we had a neighbor who could have been modeled on Nestor. His name was Butch Harris and he was an ace. Like Nestor, he was handy at everything. He advised us on the ins and outs of village life, the family feuds, where to shop and he joined in the painting of the exterior of the house. One Saturday evening, we went off to a party, leaving him hard at work with his paint brush. We protested that he shouldn't work on our house while we left to enjoy ourselves.

"I like doing it," he declared. "Go have a good time." That's the sort of good neighbor he was, kind, generous, always ready with his booming laugh. He was a fixture around the village. Everybody knew Butch. We learned how the village worked. There was a fire department manned by volunteers. There was a single cop, Uncle Harry, who took a relaxed approach to petty traffic crimes and teenage pranks. He was backed up by part-timers, some of them from the NYPD earning a bit of extra money. The mayor was always around, keeping an eye on things.

There were two libraries, one in Cold Spring and the other in neighboring Garrison, only 10-minutes away from the village. Plus, there was a system under which readers could order books from the dozens of libraries up and down the Hudson Valley without charge.

Coming to Cold Spring from Manhattan was like struggling through turbulent rapids and shooting out into placid welcoming waters although, as we discovered, there was movement in the depths. My goodness, cars actually stopped and drivers waved pedestrians jay walking across Main Street.

Cold Spring, slogan, "Where the Country Begins," had its legends. First was the dubious story that it got its name when George Washington drank from a stream there and commented that it was refreshingly cold. Historians could not find any documentation to support the theory but never mind. During the Civil War, Abe Lincoln was also supposed to have visited the village to inspect an arms-manufacturing factory but, again, there was no record of it. Call it wishful history.

Another story was that in the 1950s the Ku Klux Klan had a klavern in Cold Spring and neighboring Nelsonville. The white sheeted bigots were said to have picked up their shot guns when they heard that blacks were marching from Beacon up the river to protest something or other in Cold Spring. The klan members were said to have taken up positions at windows overlooking the streets to repel the invaders but the marchers turned back. Unbelievable, you say, and so do I. Nonetheless, the village was almost 100% white, with any dark skinned visitors getting a quick glance. The school had a sprinkling of blacks and Asians but nothing like the diversity of New York City.

. And there was a weekly newspaper, unique to my mind, The Putnam County News and Recorder, a big name for a little paper. Its slogan at that time was 120 Years Old But New Every Wednesday. It was not so much a newspaper as a local notice board. The editor would print any letter, never mind what it was about so long as it avoided personal attacks, as well as any report offered to him by locals. A newcomer who took over the paper years later, described it as "quaint" before utterly changing it.

The village emerged on the national scene in the mid-1800s because it was selected by a West Point graduate, Robert Parker Parrott, for a foundry where, as superintendent, he created and manufactured artillery pieces that helped the North win the Civil War. His cannons were used at many of the great battles and sieges of that horrific conflict. Today, as a memorial, a miniature version of his guns stands on Cold Spring's waterfront, its barrel pointing across the river at West Point. One of the village streets is named for him and the site of the long-abandoned foundry is being restored. An inn on the edge of Cold Spring is believed to have been owned by Parrott when it was a residence.

He could not have found a more charming location to produce his engines of destruction and death. Standing on the eastern bank of the Hudson, the village and its main street sloped down to the water while forested highlands surround it on all sides, indeed including steep hills, ambitious to be mountains, on the far bank of the river. The hills and their trails were marvelous for hiking.

At Cold Spring, the Hudson looks tranquil enough but its tidal currents and whirl pools could be lethal. Locals as well as visitors have drowned in its depths. A few miles downriver, directly across from the massive stonework of West Point's main buildings, stands the tiny hamlet of Garrison Landing where the academy's ferry docks so that cadets can catch trains to Manhattan and the highest of jinks. As alluring as anywhere in creation, it was used in the filming of Barbara Streisand's movie, Hello Dolly, and because of its charm weddings are sometimes held at the little gazebo overlooking the water. It became one of our favorite places to relax and we were surprised, though not disappointed, that more people didn't join us.

To house the hundreds of workers who came to Cold Spring to labor at the foundry, cottages were swiftly built but not so hastily that they could not survive into modern times. Probably our cottage was put up for foundry workers or the auxiliaries who served them. Many are brightly and cheerfully painted in the Mediterranean style. Over the years, the village had become more cosmopolitan and perhaps some of the newcomers were familiar with Mediterranean countries.

Now some houses are occupied by weekenders or commuters who take the train every day to New York City. On the road out of town, 9D, stands a well-tended group of townhouses reserved for old people. Students at the local school, who know they will never grow old, call the residences "Wrinkle Ridge," affectionately I hope but doubt. The village's placid week-day routine is shattered nowadays on Saturdays and Sundays when tourists pour in, sometimes to the disgust of the residents but not to the shopkeepers. When we arrived, a number of the shop fronts on Main Street were closed and shuttered as if Cold Spring, unable to find a role for itself, was quietly dying. That changed when antique stores started to arrive as did families fleeing New York City. With them came an improving economy.

To us, compared to Manhattan, it was a vastly different world, another America. If you were awake for some reason at 3 or 4 a.m. in the slumbering village, you sometimes could hear the melancholy hoot of a locomotive or a freighter making its way up or down the Hudson Valley. It was somehow comforting to know that others were awake and, to me, poignant and very American. It made me think of a locomotive pushing its implacable way across the western plains while on a bluff an Indian sat on his pony and watched stony-faced the alien machine take his land away from him.

This was the appealing Victorian village to which Tony's mother came together with some of her favorite antique furniture. From the start, although this was a country village not entirely dissimilar to the ones she knew in England, I don't think she was comfortable. When I took her for a walk along Main Street, just around the corner from our house, she was introduced to another woman who immediately called her by her first name, Ethel. She was astonished. In England, she said, nobody used a first name on initial acquaintanceship. Stuffy, perhaps. That sort of intimacy only came after months, if not years, of knowing somebody and being given subtle permission. Oh, dear.

Tony took her to see Boscobel, a not-so-old mansion moved in its entirety to Cold Spring from downstate by its owners, the Readers Digest originators and editors. It was open to visitors for a small charge. She was surprised that anybody could be interested in such a recent building of no great historical interest. Oh, dear. Her home in England had been near Blenheim Palace, built in the 1700s and rivaling Buckingham Palace in its splendor. Blenheim's acreage was even more spacious than that of the palace in London. It was the birthplace of Winston Churchill, following a long line of English aristocrats. But she was a game old lady and did her best to fit in. She got on well with Butch and Gert Harris next door and she loved the children, although she could have spoiled them more which as everybody knows is the job of a grandmother. She was a great reader and the small Cold Spring library was only a 15-minute walk away.

She had had a tough life, growing up during World War 1, enduring the bombing and hardships of World War 11, coping with austerity after the war, losing her oldest son when he was only 32, and then her husband, with Tony away in America.

The problem arose after she had been with us a few years. She had heart trouble and was taken to the local hospital. She spent a couple of nights there, was treated and, when released, came home with a bill for thousands of dollars. She was bewildered. In England, of course, with the National Health Service there would have been no charge. Unlike the situation in America, it was assumed that the country was responsible for the welfare of its citizens. Hard-charging right wingers contemptuously called the U.K. a nanny state. But what was wrong with that? Nannies were generally admirable people as long as they didn't spend too much time on the phone in front of the children.

The prospect of future illnesses and future astronomical bills frightened all of us. Wales came to the rescue. My sister, Sally, in Chepstow, heard of our plight and she had a suggestion. There was a pleasant home for old folks close to the shops in the town and Sally would be able to help deal with any problems. The home was subsidized by the government to some extent—oh, how terrible to live in a country where they took care of their sick and their old—and Tony's mom had enough to cover the gap. Sally made the arrangements in Wales and Tony took his mother, together with some of her best-loved furniture, back to live in a country she had never really left and with her own kind. She would be back in the embrace of the BBC and surrounded by the attitudes of people she understood. Sally's daughter, Esther, was particularly thoughtful, visiting the home whenever she could.

I watched the old lady leave with a dash of envy. My bonds with the U.K. and with Wales were perhaps attenuated by then but they remained unbroken.

The boys were settled in at the local school which, although not as demanding as the school they would have attended in Manhattan, was good enough. Now mostly on my own, I had the days to fill. I had started a business called Creative Types with Ruth Eisenhower—yes, a member, if distant, of the celebrated Eisenhower family—one of the good friends I had made in Cold Spring. We prepared resumes for locals, typed letters, designed advertisements, helped a neighbor, David Barnhardt, keep the words in order for his Barnhardt Dictionary Companion. I also made some pocket money constructing picture frames for a map and picture dealer in our earthen-floored basement.

With summer and school holidays approaching, though, we made plans for a vacation that would allow us to see more of the country and its neighbor to the north. Sometimes I had thought idly of Canada, with its quieter, more modest and civilized character, as a compromise between America and the U.K. Might be worth a look. We headed north for Montreal. Crossing the border, the Canadian officials gave us a smiling welcome. In Montreal, we rode the big wheel, enjoyed delicious food, splendid old buildings and friendly people. Until one day we were strolling on the streets when we thought we should take a ride on the subway. Tony stopped a young man and asked politely, "If you please, where's the nearest subway station?"

"I don't speak English," he said, oozing hostility, before stalking off. With my detective instincts at full alert I pegged him as a French-Canadian of the anti-English persuasion. But shouldn't he have said something like, "Je ne parle pas Anglais"? Not all Canadians, it seemed, were eager to please. Perhaps I should stop thinking idly.

Years later, the twins said they would love a return visit to Canada. We were happy to agree in the belief that the angry young French-Canadian who didn't speak English except when he was rebuffing the non-French would have moved on. We again had a good time and it was only later that we realized the boys' motive. In Montreal, at 18, they could drink beer like adults, unlike silly America where you could die for your country at 18 but drinking a beer was forbidden until three years later.

During that earlier vacation, our next goal was the Thousand Islands region of upstate New York where Tony wanted to introduce the children to an old friend, Fred Exley, who had written an ecstatically reviewed book, "A Fan's Notes" the first of a trilogy, which became something of a cult favorite among college students. It won literary prizes and was compared to The Great Gatsby. James Dickey said it was written with "brilliance and insight." Kurt Vonnegut said the book was "beautiful, one of a kind." But

Tony thought Fred's greatest prize was that he was accepted by his literary heroes like Styron and Penn Warren who talked with him on equal terms. Tony played a minor role in the semi-autobiographical work, appearing as a decorated ex-British commando, which he was not, who had moved from paper to paper across America in a restless search for something or other. I liked Fred, something of a lost soul. Sadly, his two later books, though somewhat similar to "A Fan's Notes," were received more harshly. It would have been better, we thought, if his first book had been received quietly, his second with admiration and his last with hosannas. He would have been climbing up instead of falling down. We had heard that he was drinking more than was good for him. Still, we had phoned and alerted Fred to our approach and he had expressed enthusiasm at the idea of a reunion.

He was living in a small upstairs apartment on bucolic property owned by long-time friends of his who greeted us warmly. They were nice people who were concerned about Fred and took care of him. They suggested that Tony should go up, say hello, have a chat and bring him down to meet the twins.

When Tony found him, Fred was not just drunk. He was a gibbering, slobbering, out-of-control drunk, hardly able to speak. Tony was shattered. Starting off as drinking companions in Albany, NY, they had kept in touch down the years. Tony had exulted over Fred's initial success and mourned his later literary downturn. When Fred telephoned, he sometimes sounded tipsy with a slurred voice but he never had been in this bad a condition. Tony knew that trying to introduce the twins to him in his state was impossible. Wondering if Fred had gone over the edge in some way because of our expected visit, we drove south feeling sad and bewildered. Fred died not long after.

Next stop: Cooperstown which in any language meant baseball. The boys were awestruck by all the memorabilia available for their viewing pleasure and by the pretty little ball field in the center of town. We stood behind one dugout to watch some youngsters play a game in the bright sunshine. Very soon we had to persuade, or drag, the kids away. The language coming unchecked from the dugout was appalling. The young players gathered there were displaying their machismo by using some of the foulest language I've ever heard. Goodbye Cooperstown.

The next year, Tony and family were invited by a reporter at the News to take a vacation in rooms she owned in a motel complex on the Jersey shore for a very reasonable charge. We accepted and drove down with a school friend of the boys, Justin, the son of a Cold Spring physician. The beach was splendid and, more than that, there was a large swimming pool in the motel grounds although there was something of a mystery surrounding it.

There were other children spending the summer at the motel and, of course, they used the pool. But whenever the twins and Justin jumped in, the other kids would pull away from them and leave the pool as if from the plague. If our trio tried to talk to them, the resident youngsters would be called away by their mothers. Robert, David and Justin were puzzled. What was wrong with them? Why were they the untouchables? They weren't much upset, however, because it meant that they always had the pool to themselves while all the wives and their kids watched them play from their deck chairs with a touch of malevolence.

We wondered if, because Justin was clearly Asian, the motive was raw racism. Not so.

Much later, long after the vacation, we learned the answer from a writer whose subject was the criminal underworld. The problem was that we weren't Mafia. It seems that this motel was where chieftains of the mob dumped their families for the summer while they got on with their murderous business in town. Orders had been left with the Mafia wives: Have no contact whatsoever with anybody you don't know, anybody not signed up with the mob. Never, ever talk to others. Perhaps the mob guys feared our innocent looking kids splashing in the pool were wired-up FBI agents in disguise. In the gangster world, I suppose, anything was possible. What a country.

CHAPTER THIRTEEN

Back in Cold Spring, I occasionally shopped at a high-ceilinged, spacious store on Main Street called The Country Goose. Mainly it offered kitchenware, pots and pans. knives and forks, interesting stuff like that, so essential for Cold Spring's foodies. I became friendly with the owner, Betsy, who seemed to enjoy herself behind the counter. Betsy asked me one day if I would be interested in buying the store. Her husband's company had assigned him to a new position in the mid-West and they had to move almost immediately. They would have to sell the store and they needed a quick sale.

I was intrigued. After talking it over with Ruth Eisenhower, we decided to make a joint offer which Betsy accepted. Suddenly we were shopkeepers. Betsy left almost immediately with no time to try to educate us in the arcane art of running a store. We knew nothing. We didn't know about sales taxes, how to order goods for the shelves, how to analyze customers and help them find what they wanted. We didn't know what we were doing. Betsy, for some reason, was reluctant to hand over the names of the vendors she had ordered from which meant that we had to look at all the merchandize in the store to locate the names of the manufacturers. This we did, in between dealing with the Creative Types business. We called every name we could locate to ask how we set about reordering their products.

We did discover that every so often we would have to go to Manhattan to select items likely to appeal to our lucky customers at trade shows, mostly at the Javits Center. Who was going to man, or woman, the counter while we were away? "I will," said Ruth's husband, David, an idealistic professor on vacation from his downstate college. Off we went, leaving him in control of the Country Goose.

When we returned we found that David had done a good job, selling some items and carefully making a record of them. Good work, David. But then we noticed something. The prices he had charged for his sales were far below the listed prices.

"Oh," he said, "I thought you were charging far too much for them. So I lowered the prices quite a bit. The customers were really appreciative." Goodbye, David.

Next up in our absence was Tony. He had a hard time. He didn't know where the requested items were on the shelves. He didn't know the prices. The sales tax requirement baffled him. "I did a lot of bowing and scraping, yes, ma'am, no ma'am, all that stuff," he said. "But some of the customers did get a bit irritated. In fact, one of them, as she left, said, "If I were your wife, I wouldn't let you run a hot dog stand, let alone a retail store." Goodbye, Tony.

At the beginning, we weren't much better. Salvation came in the form of a veteran salesman, Norm Jacobs, representing an outfit called Fox Run, who sat us down and gave us a 101 course in the profundities of retail sales. With his kind help we eventually got the hang of it.

Best of all was dear Fran, a long-time villager. We met because one of her kids was at school with ours and she heard I was looking for help in the store when I had to be elsewhere. She had no experience behind the counter but she said she couldn't be worse than David Eisenhower and Tony and she got that right. She was terrific. She was quick-witted, cheerful and very funny. She worked with me for years and sometimes still does. At one time or another, all her daughters did their time at the counter, too.

. For me it was fun. I in particular enjoyed meeting and gossiping with customers. Most of them were receptive to chitchat, a joke and a laugh.

Ruth was less enthusiastic about dealing with customers. She was more interested in Creative Types while my raging ego told me that I should be in complete charge. We made a deal. Tony and I would buy her out and I would be solely in charge. As the boss, I was concerned about the welfare of Main Street which was slowly recovering from a business downturn which had left some stores with boarded up windows. The Goose was a neighbor of the weekly paper, The Putnam County News, and I noticed that a group of teenagers had formed the bad habit of gathering on the paper's stoop and shouting insults at passersby, especially if they looked like visitors to the village.

I went out and delivered a tongue-lashing. Surly and defiant they wandered off.

A couple of days later during the night-time hours, a brick was hurled through our big display windows. I wonder who could have done that.

Among our early visitors was, of all people, silver-haired Steve Ross, the emperor of the ever-expanding Warner Bros. When he came in, I looked up at him in surprise and said, "D'you remember me?" He smiled and said, "Of course. How are you, Leonora?" Ross was brilliant at remembering names of people he had met for a couple of minutes. Before he could escape into the aisles, I gave him a hug. Ross was very tall so my face landed up against his chest. He smelled lovely. He spent some money, too. But his real motive for visiting our little village was the gallery of antique stores that had recently opened. These stores, leading the way in the resurrection of Main Street, attracted male visitors who browsed and bargained for antiques while their bored wives and sweethearts slipped away to spend money in the shops. Goodie.

Another drop-in was rocker Axel Rose who bought something for his aunt. Also Martha Stewart who examined everything very closely indeed.

The wife of singer-songwriter Don McLean (American Pie and Vincent} came in, bought some things and presented her credit card. It was rejected, not once but twice and three times. She was upset. I called Visa or whoever it was and they said, "That card is cancelled. You must take it from the customer and destroy it immediately."

"I'll do no such thing." I said. I knew the McLeans were living in Cold Spring and you don't treat local customers like that. Her husband wandered in during all this and said, "What's going on?" We explained.

"Put me through to the card company," he said and set about sorting it out. It turned out that the card had not been used for months and months, even years, so the company had cancelled it. Now they thought it had been stolen and the thief was using it. McLean persuaded them he was who he said he was, not though by singing American Pie, and the card was legalized.

Actor Kevin Kline, a local at weekends, came in and joined our coffee club—buy 10 pounds and get one free. Another three pounds, Mr. Kline and you get another free one. I really pushed the club idea with a tea club, a tea pot club, a toy club and it worked. People came in and said, "Am I up to ten pounds of coffee yet?" as if it were a lottery. At one point, Paul Newman came to briefly occupy a rented house in Garrison, not so much for the scenery as for the film, "Nobody's Fool," he was making in nearby Beacon. Many nights he would dine at our favorite Cold Spring restaurant, Riverview. He would slip in through a side door and sit with his back turned to other diners as if worried they would bother him. They never did, at least while we were there. He never shopped at the Country Goose.

Dar Williams, the song writer and singer of pop folk became a customer. Over the years, a number of new residents arrived, many from Brooklyn, so that the village became a sort of Brooklyn on the Hudson. Also, for some reason, Brits started coming to live in Cold Spring, commuting to Manhattan, or just to visit. To satisfy their every desire I stocked Marmite which became quite a seller although the expression of the faces of Americans when they first smelled it was a hoot worthy of use in a horror movie. Also Cadbury's chocolate (thank goodness for real chocolate—I became my own best customer} English biscuits, Ah Bisto! for gravy, Scottish shortbread, until I began to rival our friend, Peter Myers, and his English store in Greenwich Village.

On the important matter of chocolate, I refused to allow Hershey's into the store. As I wrote in a piece for Atlantic magazine on-line, "To me it had a coarser aftertaste than Cadbury's. Almost waxy. Had my grandmother eaten a Hershey bar she would have raised her Edwardian eyebrows in distaste."

Help seemed to be on the way with the announcement that Hershey's had won the rights to produce Cadbury's in America. Probably I was one of the first to buy the Hershey/Cadbury's chocolate and one of the first to be disappointed. It did not taste the same as the English Cadbury's.

On a trip back to the U.K., I picked up some Cadbury's bars and brought them back to America to hold a blind test with some American friends. Results were mixed. While a few tasters preferred Hershey's, they all loved the taste of Cadbury's. "Not as sweet," was the main comment, followed by "Cadbury's seems creamier and smoother" and "Wow, is this what chocolate should really taste like?"

I found other noble European brands that appealed, Belgian, Spanish, Italian and French. The only American products that I would allow across the doorstep of the Country Goose were Lake Champlain Chocolates of Vermont and the locally produced Gourmetibles. But Cadbury's was the best of all of them.

Why did people come to Cold Spring? Perhaps it was because it was a throwback to Victorian times without the horse manure on Main Street. Drivers traveling north or south cruised by on Route 9 a few miles to the east, leaving sleepy Cold Spring to its old fashioned architecture and peaceful atmosphere. No used car lots, no McDonalds, no Burger Kings, no Taco Bells none of the sprawling franchises that had taken over just about every town in America.

Anne Lawrence was a local attorney who liked her coffee decaffeinated so I was upset when I realized I had given her non-decaf coffee. I imagined her drinking a cup of high caffeine coffee and going into a frenzy. I frantically tried to get hold of her, leaving messages everywhere until eventually I found her and warned her off the dangerous drink. She came into the store later waving a newspaper and pointing at the headline, "Local Attorney Dies after Store Gives her Wrong Coffee." She had gone to the trouble of having a fake headline splashed across the Putnam County

News front page to give me a fright. That's the way it went in Cold Spring, a bit of fun unimaginable in other cities or towns. I loved it.

For me, it wasn't all work. At weekends when there was a rush on at the store, Fran would take over behind the counter to give me a break with the twins who on Saturday mornings played soccer. I was from the U.K. so of course I must know the rules of soccer. I was appointed a coach. Hah. My game was Rugby. I hadn't the barest idea of soccer's rules, I protested. Nonsense, they said, you're a Brit. I fell back on crying to my team: "Kick the ball, kick it!" When disputes about rules came up I would pretend I knew who was right and who was wrong. I was a Brit, wasn't I? Usually it worked because nobody else knew the rules either.

One Saturday morning, my team was on the field and after a while I called one of the kids back to the sideline to make room for one who, not selected, was watching glumly It was critical that every kid got a chance to kick the ball, kick it. But the mother of the benched youngster, wife of an FBI agent, was furious. Protesting loudly that her son was entitled to more time on the field, she stormed up to me, ignoring my attempt to explain my dastardly action. The next things I knew, she had delivered a stinging slap to my face. My goodness, assault and battery on the playing fields of Cold Spring. I was stunned but graciously didn't return the slap. No cat fights, thank you, and I didn't think of suing which showed the Americanization of Leonora had not been completed. After that, we didn't talk to each other. But the twins were good friends of the benched youngster and eventually because of them we made up and behaved like grown-ups.

Soccer didn't really appeal to the kids. I noted that after the games, the boys would find an American football and enthusiastically launch a full-contact competition between the Jets and the Giants.

Fran also took over when we went on vacation. One trip we took was to Martha's Vineyard, a favorite of ours where Tony and I had spent a winter weekend before the arrival of the twins. Back then, a fashionista at Women's Wear Daily had invited a bunch of us to fly over and stay at her parent's summer house on the island. We had a pleasant enough time until the night of our departure when the young hostess presented us with a bill "to cover my costs" What? I was furious but I had the answer. I opened my purse and presented her with a much larger bill for the wines and spirits Tony and I had bought for the household on the night of our arrival. Checkmate. We sent her to Coventry and on the flight home she sat by herself, probably counting her money.

We should have known. This was the same girl that for some reason beyond me now we had given a quite expensive piece of jewelry. Friends reported they had seen the little trinket for sale on a table when the recipient decided to sell off some of her belongings to any cronies she could corral. I was surprised she still had any friends. She was not a gift giver; she was a gift seller. No wonder her family could afford a weekend house on the Vineyard.

Curious about our new life in a one traffic light village, David English, now Sir David, came to visit. After a stroll around the village, we sat down to dinner—I had become a decent cook, using a recipe as a basis and then becoming seriously adventurous with additional touches. After a day in the store with the usual ration of difficult customers, the enjoyment of cooking became my way of relaxing

Between mouthfuls, David told a tale that in a minor way foreshadowed what was to come to Cold Spring. It revolved around the time when he was moving swiftly up the ladder of British journalism but also determined to have enough capital that in a head-to-head policy disagreement or a crisis of conscience he could walk away from any newspaper. To this end, he and his wife, Irene, established a laundromat in the London suburb where they then lived and they launched a free newspaper supported financially by advertisements. Both did well. The joke was that the elegantly beautiful Irene put her back out carrying so many heavy bags of coins from the laundromat to the bank.

Out of the nowhere, Rupert Murdoch, not long in London where he was buying everything in sight, contacted David and said bluntly, "I want to buy your little paper."

"Not for sale," said David, startled that the Australian newcomer had even heard of his paper.

"If you don't sell, I'll put you out of business," said Murdoch. "You know I have the money. I'll start up a rival sheet and pour resources into it and I'll leave you in the dust, the paper bankrupt."

David, a realist, gave it some thought, then surrendered. "Murdoch wasn't screwing me entirely," he recalled. "His offer was reasonable. Still, I didn't enjoy being intimidated like that." This was before Murdoch proved he was a great newspaperman by putting a bared bosom every day on Page Three of his Sun newspaper.

"Charming," I said.

"Intimidation?" Tony said. "I'll tell a story of Murdoch trying to intimidate. During a newspaper strike, a number of us out-of-work hacks got together, secured financial backing and produced a very successful strike paper with reporters and ad-men from the Times and Daily News. We were paid at union rates. The strike went on and on, the money poured in to our financial backers. I'm talking thousands and thousands of dollars. Then a rival paper appeared, called The Metro. Very quickly the rumor went around that it was Murdoch, owner of the strike-bound New York Post, who was behind it., If true, it was highly embarrassing for Murdoch because he was supposed to be closely allied with the owners of the Times and News in confronting the unions and here he was secretly breaking ranks for his own benefit.

"I called him at his weekend retreat in upstate New York and put it to him. In less than a minute, he managed to lie to me and to try to intimidate me. He flatly denied any connection with the new paper. "I would be very careful what you write, young man," he said menacingly. "Oh, I'm always very careful what I write," I assured him but he had hung up. A week or so later, the truth emerged. Murdoch had financed The Metro. Unfortunately for him, the strike didn't last much longer and his paper never really got traction. Probably he lost money together with another tatter to his fading reputation for integrity."

"What's it all about, then, Alfie?" I asked, fascinated.

"It's not the money. It's power," said David, who, as a potentate of Fleet Street, knew something about power.

"Control," Tony said. "Control is everything for Murdoch and people like him.".

CHAPTER FOURTEEN

My chief joy in running the store was the customers. You never knew who might wander in and what they might want. Some were doleful, resisting any attempt to cheer them up. Some were out-of-uniform home-sick West Point cadets. Some were killing time until their train was due. Some walked in talking on their cell phones and never stopping. Some were fun, a delight because they laughed at my tired old jokes. "It's ten dollars to look and 20 dollars to touch anything." Then there was David Duffy who claimed he was a novelist and still does in spite of evidence to the contrary. He would come in for his coffee and cheerfully spray insults at me, complaining about my surly attitude, the slovenly look of the store and its rip-off prices before leaving with a chortling farewell "See you next week if you haven't been arrested for cheating your customers." Some spent money as if their name was Rockefeller until I felt I had to rein them in. If I could make them laugh I was content. Those who responded to my chatter often had interesting stories to tell.

At first I had to close the store at 3 p.m. when the boys left school looking for something to eat.

After that they would vanish to play with schoolmates or go exploring the woods and fields around the village. In those days, there was no worry about child predators or any other harm. Maybe there should have been. We were settling in although we would never be Cold Springers. For that you would have to be born into a family going back generations. Still we were accepted into village life which went on in its somnolent old ways.

There were changes. A few years after we arrived, Bob Ingram, who owned the Putnam County News, sold it to his business manager, Brian O'Donnell, although the change in ownership brought no difference in its presentation whatsoever. As a journalist, Tony laughed at the amateurish approach and invited O'Donnell to lunch to discuss what might be done to improve it. He offered to cover town and village meetings in his spare time, no charge. O'Donnell said, fine.

But when Tony moved on to suggest some changes in the paper, O'Donnell shook his head. "I'm not a journalist," he said. "But I like the paper the way it is." It remained the way it was although O'Donnell had one fine journalistic instinct. He believed in free speech and he would publish almost any letter from readers as long as they weren't obscene or declaring that the mayor was a bigamist who held up banks and defrauded widows and orphans to finance his orgies. It was the best-read section of the paper.

As for covering the community meetings, Tony did his best but found they were far more difficult than reporting his usual agenda of sensational murders or civil rights marches or earthquakes or splashy trials. "The thing is you had to know the details of village life to make any sense of what was being discussed," he said ruefully. "I didn't. I would have to go to speakers after the meetings to try to understand the subtleties and nuances of what was being said and decided. I gave up."

In contrast, I rather liked the gray, boring old paper that never, ever raised its voice. If it stumbled across a scoop, not that it ever did except for one startling announcement about the paper's future, the Putnam County News and Recorder wouldn't know what to do with it. It was like a loveable old carthorse comfortably plodding along a trail that it had known for years, a horse that had no ambition to be a sleek muscled racer or to trot into a show ring to display its skills. Nobody knew if O'Donnell had any political views because there were never any editorials in the paper. It made the New York Times look like a screaming, rabid tabloid and I was happy to sell it at the Country Goose.

It was a blessed relief from the blaring headlines of the daily papers and the shouting radio voices and the "investigative reporters" of TV who proudly announced they had discovered something or other that was of no importance at all. Eventually, Tony came to agree with me. The old paper, laugh at it as you might, perfectly suited this little village, enjoying the slow rhythm of country life for decades. Cold Spring knew what it was and was content. When Steven Spielberg wanted to flood it with cameras and hoopla to film some scenes for his movie, The War of the Worlds, Cold Spring said he should try somewhere else even if Mr. Spielberg might have brought a lot of money into the village.

Actually, it was far more complicated than that. The Spielberg invasion was defeated mostly by one man, Donald Lusk. Lusk was as much a fixture of Cold Spring as the village office or the view across the river of the massive bulk of Storm King mountain (what a marvelous name), or house painter Steve Lindstedt's sense of humor which led him to hang a cutout of a life-size overalled painter clinging to a ledge on Steve's building at the corner of Main and Rock Sts.

The eyes of connoisseurs of the local paper's letters to the editor column always brightened when they spotted a letter from Donald Lusk who never hesitated to express his robust views on life and, more importantly, the village. He was quirky, difficult, funny, stubborn, opinionated and remarkably well-read for a not-often-employed carpenter who sometimes rode the village garbage pick-up truck. I didn't know him well but I became fond of him and his readiness to take on anybody, however lofty. In a village in the U.K. he would have fitted in perfectly because every village over there had to have a character. Although he was only in his 30s when I first came across him, he reminded me a bit of my father who also could be peculiar. Donald relished words and used them deftly. It was in the family. Tony would sometimes commute on the train to Manhattan that also carried Donald's wife, Wanda, to work. Tony never saw her without a book.

I think Donald believed his role in life was as a defender of Cold Spring where his family had lived for more than a hundred years. In letters to the editor he called the waterfront "magical" and objected to change unless it was something that met his hard won approval. He was always on the look-out for greedy commercial interests that wanted to exploit the village. He wasn't very fond of sightseers, either.

His house, not the most cared for, stood at the bottom end of Main Street only a few buildings away from the Hudson and the concrete dock used by tourists to survey the river and beyond it the forested hills of the West Point academy. So he had every reason to give much thought to Hollywood's decision to use Cold Spring as a background. That would definitely change things.

Thumbs down, sort of.

In a letter to the paper, Donald complained that the project was being settled in back room deals with no participation of residents He suspected that the money Spielberg would bring in would not go to the general benefit of Cold Spring. "Paramount (Pictures)" he wrote, "has done all it can to keep us all guessing as to the facts and figures by dealing with residents individually, trying to work out separate deals and causing animosity among my neighbors."

Then he got down to the nub which suggested that, being human, he was not entirely selfless. "It's also been said that Paramount is going to put a blue shield in front of my house and impose a different house in its place due to the condition of my home. Paramount, why don't you help me fix the front of my home, it's not that bad." At one point, Donald had set about upgrading his house but ran out of money with the task half-way done and left it unfinished.

Eventually Spielberg gave up on Cold Spring and sent his cameras and crew into a village higher up the Hudson. I suspect that Hollywood just got impatient with all the palaver, and the fact that the river was so silted a dock would have to be built to accommodate the ship they planned to use, and said, "The hell with them, we'll go where we and our money are welcome."

While Donald had his loyal followers, he was not popular with some of the residents, particularly those who might have benefited from an influx of film-maker's dollars. My store could have been among them but I had no quarrel with Donald. He was just doing his thing.

Donald was also a veteran of a long-running battle over the future of a disused lumber yard at the rear of his house which directly overlooked the waters of the Hudson. A developer (Donald liked to call developers, greasy} wanted to tear down the ramshackle lumber yard buildings and throw up condominiums on the site in an area that Donald felt was the beating heart of historic Cold Spring. He was not alone. Other locals living close to the picturesque riverfront also objected to the size of the planned condos and the density of people that would be crammed into them. In fact, during the fight with Paramount Pictures, Donald suggested Hollywood should buy the lumber yard and build a youth-community center or an extension of the local museum. "Take the most precious piece of land in the history of Cold Spring," he told village officials, "and for once think about the residents of Cold Spring first over the quick buck of a developer." Dream on, Donald.

In his battle over the condos, Donald put up home-made signs on his porch expressing his disgust at the planned desecration of his precious waterfront. Village officials objected to the signs and the mayor ordered the police to remove them. Donald paid a fine for violating the zoning laws but, although he had very little money, Donald had only just begun to fight. Through the ACLU, he found a law firm across the river in Orange County, Thornton, Bergstein & Ullrich, which specialized in civil rights cases and they agreed to represent him.

Curious about lawyers ready to accept a client with little money, Tony called them and connected with his attorney, Steven Bergstein. "We knew he had no money," said Bergstein. "But he managed to come up with about $200. We went ahead because we knew we couldn't lose with this clear violation of the free speech amendment and we didn't. The judge decided for us."

Donald left no doubt about his political inclinations. When he arrived at his attorney's offices he saw that the building was also the headquarters of the local Republican Party. He didn't want to enter the enemy camp until persuaded that the law firm was more of the left, than the right.

"He was a fanatical fan of the Beatles," said Bergstein, "and when he saw a photograph of George Harrison that I had put up in the men's room he knew he was in the right place." The legal complications lasted more than two years but at the end, Cold Spring—or its insurance company—had to pay $50,000 in legal costs for losing. "Donald despised the mayor and he was so happy that he had won," said Bergstein. "He was a cool guy but also an emotional one. He was fun to work with. It's trouble-makers like him, not ordinary people who stay out of trouble, who protect the liberties of everybody."

During this same period, Donald decided to run for mayor, complaining that Anthony Phillips, a true gritty ex-marine, had held the office for too long at 12 years. I also liked Phillips, who it's certain loved Cold Spring as much as Donald did, just in different ways. The mayor brushed Donald away like an annoying fly. When a friend filed the necessary papers on Donald's behalf, the mayor lodged an objection that the Lusk petition had given an inaccurate address. The young insurgent had so little chance of winning that I wondered why the mayor bothered. If Donald was excluded, his few supporters certainly wouldn't vote for Phillips. The county board of elections upheld the objection immediately and declared Donald's petition "null and void." American democracy in action.

It struck me that Donald Lusk, stubborn, taking on the big guys, ornery, difficult, going against the tide, represented the best of America. He died aged only 50. Too soon for me and a hard core of his supporters in Cold Spring. We need more cranky Donald Lusks, if only for my entertainment.

As for the lumber yard condos, a compromise was reached. Instead of the feared condominiums, a row of attractive townhouses sprang up, smart, well-maintained and not out of place alongside the Hudson. One anti-condo campaigner said later, "We didn't get everything we wanted but they're certainly better than the abandoned lumber yard." I think Donald would have been satisfied.

CHAPTER FIFTEEN

I had turned my back on Manhattan except for the occasional trip to trade shows. I had become so countrified that when my sisters or my friends arrived in New York for a visit from the U.K. I would insist that we meet for dinner at the Oyster Bar in Grand Central Terminal. I would take the train down, dine at the Oyster Bar without even seeing the streets of Manhattan, then board the train back to Cold Spring. If the visitors brought their children or we had the twins with us, the kids would delight in the architectural quirk outside the doors of the Oyster Bar which allowed you to whisper in one corner of the corridor and be heard in another corner yards away.

Tony was still commuting to Manhattan every day but he was struggling with disturbing changes at his paper, the Daily News. "It's been taken over by editors who spent too much time in journalism school and too little on the streets," he said. "They have too much ambition and too little talent." The paper was losing circulation at an alarming speed.

That was when David English reappeared in our lives. Once again, he offered Tony a job, this time in the New York bureau of the London Daily Mail. Tony quickly accepted. It meant that we would be staying in America, at least for a while. His first out-of-town trip for the Mail was to Virgin Gorda, where we had married, to cover the visit by Princess Diana, her marriage in tatters, to Richard Branson's private little island.

At the store, I was learning every day—and still am. I learned that it was easy to make friends with Americans, the UPS guy, the mailman, the checkout girls at the little supermarket, Craig and Scotty at the garage and, of course, Donny at the liquor store. Not forgetting Seth, who made bag pipes. It was odd. In the U.K., bagpipes and kilts were very much a Scottish thing. In the U.S. the Irish had pirated the custom.

I learned that the best way to bring in customers was to be cheerful and friendly and helpful without trying to push sales so that they came back as much for the atmosphere as for the items on the shelves. I learned that start-up companies like Green Mountain Coffee and Yankee Candles were happy to have me as a customer until with the help of small stores like mine they became big enough to sell to large chain outlets like Target, Macy's and Bloomingdales who undercut small store prices. That was before the bullying Amazon came along and set about destroying us completely. I'll get to that.

A woman came in and started creating a gift basket for her chauffeur, selecting items from the shelves to fill it. Interesting. Soon I launched a gift basket business which became a mainstay of the store. With me, you didn't just buy a generic gift basket. You had to tell me what sort of person the recipient was, a golfer, a sports fan, a devotee of cooking, a candy-lover and I filled the basket accordingly. At Christmas when the rush was on, my sister Bridget would fly over from England to help and my friend, Diane, would organize a group of volunteers interested in learning the ins and outs of the gift basket business, would congregate in the basement to fill the orders for corporate baskets or holiday baskets, or sympathy baskets, shower baskets. We called the basement ladies our "Desperate Housewives."

Black Labrador retrievers. I adore them. Our first was Sable, followed by Tara. There was a bench immediately outside the store where they liked to sit watching the activity on Main Street. I looked out of the window one day and saw a barbarous teenage girl pushing the poor dog off the seat to make room for herself. The next day a sign was attached to the bench: This Seat Reserved for Lady Tara. It was a joke but sometimes tourists would sit down until, noticing the sign, they would hastily get to their feet, spilling apologies.

I put up signs in the window such as, "It's Difficult To Be Humble If You're Welsh" and "Thank God I'm Welsh" and was surprised by how many people came in from Cardiff or Swansea or even Newport, wanting to know, "Who's Welsh around here?" I'd put on a Tom Jones CD and we'd have a nostalgic concert. Still, I was determined not to be one of those expat ladies who sit around sipping tea and talking about "our dear Queen." There were Australians and French, and Dutch and Canadians and Irish and Brits, many of the tourists coming on the train to Cold Spring because it was the only village up the Hudson and within striking distance of Grand Central that had a station a few steps away from the village center. In earlier days, one of our best friends, the Australian, Derryn Hinch, a reporter from Melbourne who became a veteran radio and TV celebrity Down Under. I had a photograph of him taken when he was still in his teens and I liked to ask Australian customers if they recognized him. A surprising number did and they were just as surprised to find his photo in far away Cold Spring.

Not all Brits were a pleasure. The younger ones were usually fine but the older ones could be difficult, stuffy and remote. A couple came in and demonstrated how they would appear arrogant and dismissive to Americans. Because of the class system I immediately recognized them as upper middle class.

"Hello, how are you?"

"All right." (Thinks: She's only a shopkeeper and she's talking as though she's our equal).

"Did you come up on the train?"

"Yes." (Thinks: That's our business,)

"Are you having a good time?"

"Yes." (Thinks: Not right now.)

"What do you think of Cold Spring?

"It's all right." (Thinks: Not as nice as an English village.)

"Where are you from?"

"London." (Thinks: Is this an interrogation?)

"Can I help you with anything?"

"No." (Thinks: Just stop pretending to be interested in us.)

Americans wouldn't be like that, would they? Ah, here come three young women, tres chic in high heels and short skirts, almost certainly from Manhattan. Chattering, they march down the aisle and two of them vanish into the little bathroom at the back of the store, while the other one waits her turn. When they reappear at the front of the store and head for the door, I say, "Excuse me, but in England it would be considered polite to ask permission to use the bathroom. If you had, I could have told you that there's a certain trick to managing the lever on the lavatory. You have to keep it pressed down for a second or two or you get a mess."

One of them looks at me scornfully and says, "If that's your attitude, you shouldn't be running a store," before flouncing out.

When they've gone—without spending a penny except in the bathroom—I examine it. What a mess. Jammed up toilet paper is swirling around in the bowl and the water is about to spill. I clean up. Now remember, Leonora, you're a cheery soul.

The Goose also expanded into children's books and toys. That could produce mayhem when mothers came in with children out of control. The little beasts would pull toys off shelves, throw them around, break them, while the mother stood by, making no attempt to discipline the kids who probably would grow up to become mass murderers. It could take a half hour or more to restore order to the kids' corner. When, at the dinner table, I complained to Tony about the failure of American moms to control their kids he reminded me of the time we had taken the twins, then toddlers, to lunch at our favorite Chinese restaurant in Manhattan. They set about entertaining themselves by throwing bread at the other diners, mostly businessmen and women, and, in spite of our best efforts, created a noisy nuisance. The distressed manager, an old friend, said we were upsetting his customers and we would have to leave which we did. Okay, point taken. I also arranged for children's parties in the store for local families and we all had a good time.

The twins were growing up American, with American accents and American attitudes. They played formal baseball and soccer games on a field down by the river under the eyes of the organizers, adults who sometimes seemed more competitive than the kids. The better time for the boys was out of the presence of shouting grown-ups. Robert and David would phone around the village and gather their friends to play their own version of football without annoying adults telling them what to do. They became ardent fans of the Yankees and the Giants while despising the horrid New England teams. In self-defense, so that he knew what they were talking about, Tony slowly learned about American football and eventually became an enthusiast. A onetime rugby player, he offered a solution to the problem of devastating injuries suffered in American football. He believed that helmets turned players into human battering rams. In rugby, there were no helmets so an unprotected head could not be used as a weapon. Also, rugby players didn't run on and off the field all the time, spending half the 60 minute game watching from the sidelines, the wimps. Rugby players spend every 80 minutes of the game on the field, with only six substitutes allowed which mightily lessens the urge to smash opponents to the ground all the time because they have to husband their strength. Get rid of the helmets, he argued, and the number of dangerous concussions would fall as swiftly as tropical darkness. My thought was: The fans would never stand for it. They were fascinated by the violence. That's what they paid to see.

On vacations the boys had learned to swim and we discovered that the Olympic-sized swimming pool at West Point, across the Hudson, was available at certain times for youngsters living in the area. We drove them over and, under the guidance of instructors, they became pretty good swimmers.

We liked the way they made friends with outsiders, the few minorities, blacks, Asians and Hispanics, in a 90 per cent white community. As twins they were not bothered by bullies because they always had each other's backs. If a brute tried to take on Robert he would find David attacking him from the flank. They told us years later that at school they had been mocked because their parents were British. On one occasion as they were leaving the gymnasium, a fat schoolmate jeered, "Off home for our afternoon tea and scones?" David fixed him with his cold blue stare and replied, "No, because they're all in your fat ass." A teacher overheard his words and called him over. "That was very wrong of you, David," she said. "You must never call attention to another student's unfortunate physical appearance." He tried to explain what it was all about but it was like the official at a football game who doesn't see the first blow struck but does see the response and punishes the wrong player.

At one point, they connected with a black kid at school and asked if he could have a sleep-over with them. He said he would have to get his mom's permission. She came around, examined our house and its upkeep, put a finger in a little patch of dust and said she didn't think it would be a good idea. The boys were disappointed and so was their friend. We never did find out where we had fallen short.

To me, house cleaning was a drag. You dust and vacuum and polish, then you have to do the same thing again and again. BORING. The store, on the other hand, was never boring. There were always new people coming to the counter, some cheerful, some funny, some doleful, some straight-faced but many of them interesting if you got them talking.

When they were 15, we sent the boys off to a boarding school in Connecticut which in those days was almost affordable. Like most American prep schools, it was modeled on the ancient boarding schools of England like Eton and Harrow although without the weird outfits English schoolboys were forced to wear but with female students. It might have been a mistake but the kids were excited at the idea of being independent, off on their own away from mom and dad with their silly rules. After a couple of years, though, among the lessons they learned was the age-old art of hypocrisy. The administration seemed to have two jolly strict rules, both revolving around the dollar. One said that students from wealthy families that might become serious benefactors of the school should not be hassled or, God forbid, expelled. Scholarship kids, while useful to demonstrate that the students were diverse, were a little different and clearly were in need of strong discipline. The second rule said that wealthy alumnae who had a few millions to spare should be treated with caring affection.

One of the school's benefactors was a Wall Street financier, noted for taking over companies and then firing employees in the worthy American pursuit of profits. In return for his multi-million donation, he was invited to address a graduating class. His speech emphasized the over-riding importance of ideals and integrity, in the future lives of the graduating class.

The school proudly recorded the number of minority students attending. Among them while the twins were there was an American Indian student from Broken Bow (lovely name), Oklahoma, who was given a scholarship. He didn't have many pals at the school where students and staff knew who the scholarship kids were but the boys became friendly with him. So did a girl student. They knew that he came from a background of poverty and lived with an alcoholic uncle but now he had a chance to escape into a better life. Call him Ben because that wasn't his name.

Such was the situation when summer vacations came around. The twins were away visiting their many cousins in the U.K. I got a call from the girl who sounded distraught. "I don't know what to do," she said. "Ben is down in Oklahoma and he says he's not coming back to school. He's living with his drunken uncle again. I've tried on the phone to persuade him that he's throwing away his best chance at a decent life but he's so unhappy at the school that he won't consider returning."

I told her I would call the school which I did. I explained the situation to an official who said coldly, "It's vacation time. He's not at school so he's not our responsibility. There's nothing we can do."

I was angry. As a minority student Ben was a useful statistic that the school could employ to demonstrate its diversity. but now he was not the school's responsibility. I reported this to the girl who, upset, said she wanted to go down to Oklahoma for a face-to-face discussion with Ben.

I sent her some money to help pay for the trip and she later called to say that she had gone to Oklahoma but in spite of all her arguments, Ben refused to return to the school. Oh, well, there were lots more statistics where he came from.

Cold Spring and the store were fun and I enjoyed the village and its characters. I was content. The village had applied the soothing balm to my initial disillusion with America but now the boarding school demonstrated an ugly truth about the country. It pretended otherwise but there was a class system, a snobbery, based not on birth but on money. If you were wealthy you got special treatment just as noble birth in the U.K. gave you a flying start in life.

Wondering where this greed for wealth came from, I did a little research which resulted in a discovery, ignored by most Americans that would have caused the lip of Ben from Broken Bow to curl. In 1763, it seemed, London's treasury had been beggared by the French-Indian wars for which the colonists refused to pay. The Brits had had enough of these expensive wars and therefore issued a proclamation that the colonists could not cross the Appalachians to fight the Indians and steal their land. The U.K, in the role of guardians of the Indians, put a line of troops across the no-go barrier but it was impossible to stem the flood of settlers pushing west to grab the land from Ben's forefathers.

This perhaps explained a tale told by Tony. He was up near the Canadian border on a story when he met some Indians. They said they liked Brits but despised Americans.

"Why?"

"The British were good to us years ago," one said.

"What d'you mean?"

"I don't really know but the stories passed down by our forefathers were that the English tried to protect us from the Americans who were taking our land." Somebody up there on the border liked us. How nice.

Objecting to the restriction of the colonists to the east coast and to London's attempt to tax them to help pay the bill for their protection, the Americans launched the War of Independence. This was followed by the hallowed constitution written by the Founding Fathers, some of them owners of slaves. The slaves were not allowed to vote any more than were women, men without property and Indians whose land had been seized. God bless America.

None of this would have mattered much because most countries have murky histories. What made it annoying was the way Americans talked about their political system's birth as if it were somehow blessed by the Almighty

At some point as they grew up, the twins developed a fascination with military history, an obsession that lasts until today. After college, Robert decided he wanted to become an officer in the U.S. Marines. Semper Fi. He went to Albany in upstate New York where he was interviewed by an impeccably dressed marine captain for an hour or so. He then returned home to await word on his future. It never came. There was no letter to say that he had been accepted or indeed rejected. He made phone calls but got no satisfaction although the silence surely meant they didn't want him. How rude of the U.S. Marines! Also how kind of them! Only a year or so later came 9/11 and Afghanistan and Iraq. Most surely if Rob had been accepted he would have been prime meat for the wars and I would have spent my time worrying like thousands of other mothers. Love those U.S. Marines.

Instead, he went to England and joined the British Army. "Smaller but more professional," he claimed. He was assigned to the elite Household Cavalry which traced its history back to Cromwell's time. Rob was joined in the regiment by Prince Harry but, comrades in arms as they were, the prince didn't once invite him out for a drink and a chat. Bad Harry. Rob's duties focused on riding horses around London on ceremonial occasions while tourists gawked and took photographs. The cavalry, though, did not escape combat. Because horses did not fare well against AK-47s and rockets, the cavalry deployed armored vehicles for long-range reconnaissance in Iraq and Afghanistan where the unit found that their lightly-armored mounts did not fare well either against bombs buried in the roads.

Happily, Rob, who had married a London girl, finished his hitch before he could be dispatched to the wars. Love that Household Cavalry. In 2011, he was managing the night shift at a supermarket while training during the day to become a teacher. He was at work during the riots which wracked London and other cities across England. The supermarket workers were always locked in while they restocked shelves but around 1 a.m. Robert decided to take a look outside. In England, supermarkets often include gas stations and when he looked across to the pumps he saw smoke rising and then leaping flames. The pumps were alight. Security cameras later showed that a man in a hooded jacket had drenched the pumps with an accelerant and then set them on fire. Rob put in an emergency call and within five minutes the fire brigade was on the scene dousing the blaze. The firefighters told him that, given a few more minutes, the whole neighborhood, especially the supermarket, could have blown up.

The hierarchy of the supermarket chain was suitably grateful for Rob's quick, life-saving work. He was awarded vouchers worth ten pounds (about 15 dollars) although they could be spent only at stores in the chain for which he worked. Perhaps realizing that, although this surely was much appreciated, it might be considered less than munificent the supervisors sent him another letter awarding him two days off. The minor mistake was that in the letter he was addressed as "Nigel." They apologized so that was all right.

David, who was equally fascinated by the military, wisely decided he would rather read about it than actually pick up a gun. He moved down to the city and found a job which didn't demand marching around and shooting at people. Both of them had sworn they would never spend their working lives sitting in front of a computer and, so far, both have succeeded in that goal.

CHAPTER SIXTEEN

The office of the Putnam County News stood in the middle of the stores on Main Street. Donald Lusk said that his great grandfather, Frank Julian, had run a barber's shop in the building where, no doubt, juicier gossip than ever appeared in the newspaper was exchanged.

The office had a large front window and through it you could see the desk of Margaret, our friend and the friend of just about everybody else in Cold Spring, who was the paper's advertising manager. She would wave at passers-by and they would wave back.

If you wanted to see the owner, publisher and editor, Brian O'Donnell, perhaps to wield a horse whip, there he was in plain sight amid three or four staffers struggling for space in the cramped quarters. O'Donnell was not opposed to progress and he installed computers for stories to be written and pages to be laid out, together with a web site. A hands-on editor, he personally delivered his paper around Cold Spring and its surrounding hamlets, all of which were encompassed in the township of Philipstown.

Around the year 2001, a Manhattan executive and his wife paid millions of dollars for a property just outside Cold Spring which, from high atop a steep hill, commanded sensational views of the Hudson and the surrounding countryside. It looked down on the village. Their arrival for weekend visits had no immediate impact on the villages below or the Putnam County News but it would. On Sundays, with their schoolboy son, Zachary, they religiously attended the Catholic Church on a street running off Main Street. Sometimes the wife would play the organ.

I first met her when she came in to shop at the Country Goose. An attractive blonde with a forthright manner, she would buy from the shelves and quite often would order gift baskets.

She was a first rate customer who spent freely as I expect she did in other stores. Her son was a nice, well-behaved kid and, recalling the little terrors who sometimes wrecked my children's corner, I concluded she was a good mother. With me, that counted for a lot. I liked her and, being a hugger, sometimes gave her one. From gossip, I learned that her husband was Roger Ailes, the creator and chief of TV's Fox News which had made a joke of the words, "fair" and "balanced" and suffered a large deficit of nuance. I didn't admire Murdoch's Fox News which to me represented much of the worst of America, with its bullying tone, its contempt for nations that didn't support the greatest country in the world and its blatant right wing propaganda. My first reaction to Beth Ailes, Roger's third wife, was one of pity. I felt sorry for her. Fancy having to live with somebody who, like a circus owner, had recruited and run a stable of clowns such as O'Reilly, Hannity and the strange Glenn Beck who eventually became too Beckish even for Roger Ailes. They made Monty Python look like a sober commentary on modern life. Separating her from her husband's occupation, I remained friendly enough. What did it matter that her husband was who he was. It wouldn't affect me or Cold Spring.

Because I found it idiotic, I didn't watch much of Fox News but I did hear that it was complaining bitterly about "The War on Christmas." The pious Roger and his men were valiantly defending the celebration against the alleged assault by a battalion of Godless enemies. It struck me, though, that Fox's defense of the rich and disregard for the poor was hardly in accord with the precepts of gentle Jesus. It occurred to me that Roger might face some searching questions from St. Peter when he presented himself at the Pearly Gates.

Tony, who had encountered much weirdness in his career, couldn't take Fox seriously but I wondered if the reappearance in my life of Ailes, who might have set me shouting, "Nixon's the One" all those years ago, was signaling that the disillusion with America of those days would return with the Fox News chief. What did it say about Americans that so many tuned in Roger's' programs? His influence on TV went further than Fox. Trying to compete, MSNBC followed the Fox template and produced cable programs that were almost as distasteful on the left as Fox was on the right. MSNBC's guests almost always agreed 100% with the hosts. It was nothing more than political agit prop and it was boring. CNN, losing viewers while struggling to walk a moderate, middle course, appeared defensive and bland.

Anyway, Tony and I preferred humor or crime on TV. Musing once on different styles, I mentally pitted the American Seinfelds and Law and Orders against the British Fawlty Towers and Inspector Morses (no damned commercials on the British entries) and decided regretfully that American humor had the edge.

In Cold Spring, my live-and-let-live attitude prevailed until a day in 2008 when the front page of the Putnam County News and Recorder reported that, OMG, Roger had stepped in and bought the old paper. O'Donnell would remain for a short time as a consultant and then retire. At first, the PCNR remained pretty much as it always had been. But in the Spring of 2009, O'Donnell finally walked out of the shabby little office for the last time and the paper was left in the hands of Beth Ailes who had been named publisher by her husband.

Roger was welcomed to the ranks of newspaper tycoons by the daily Journal News in neighboring Westchester County which, perhaps aware of his security obsession, slyly published his home address outside Cold Spring. Roger was not amused and he retaliated. A truce was soon declared.

Big changes were ahead. Roger was making millions and he was prepared to spend them The little office in the building where Donald Lusk's great grandfather had cut hair was abandoned and the PCNR moved up Main Street to a building Roger had bought next to the firehouse. The spacious new office, completely renovated and refurbished, was sleekly elegant, quiet and attractive. It sported Tiffany-style lamps and a darkened front window which made it difficult to look in. No more waves from passers-by. At the rear, an elevator was installed so that Roger, who had failing legs, could reach the second floor without difficulty. On the façade was a balcony decorated with American flags, three of them to demonstrate that Ailes was more patriotic than ordinary people who flew a pathetic single flag.

Villagers became used to the occasional glimpse of Roger, always accompanied by burly security men, aka bodyguards or muscle. On the infrequent occasions he attended community meetings, he would be escorted by a bodyguard who occupied a seat next to his boss. At crowded meetings, there were some mutterings about a non-resident taking a seat while locals had to stand at the back but nobody had the courage to try to claim the seat.

Paranoid was the word often attached to Roger. He was said to have ordered the removal of all trees around his house so that he, his bodyguards and dogs had a 360 degree view of any leftist assault teams preparing to rush the house. He also was reported to have bought most of the half-dozen houses on his little road presumably so that they could not be used as staging posts for an assault on him. That was in addition to the numerous cameras that would capture movements by the attackers as they locked and loaded their weapons and deployed to mount their action. It was not known if there were defenses against artillery fire.

These matters did not come up when Roger talked at some length about Cold Spring to the New Yorker magazine. In that 2011 interview, he said, "We understand that because of my job, and because of Fox News, some people are just not going to like me. That's it. There's nothing I can do about it." Er, actually there was something. He could turn Fox News into a legitimate news organization. The banzai leftists, their motives gone, would be forced to put down their weapons, disband and leave Roger free of fear.

But it was the newspaper that caused the greatest ruckus. Roger brought in 25-year-old Joe Lindsley, a Southerner from a wealthy family, who would act as editor and enforcer of right-wing political correctness. Conservative? Check. Catholic? Check. Hard worker? Check. Aggressive? Check, Provocateur? Check. Loyal? Check (for the moment).

The splashy headlines that had succeeded Brian O'Donnell's modest approach and the blatant conservative tilt of the paper dismayed me. The paper was no longer quietly unique. It was just another weekly laid out as ordained by the journalism schools. Right wing editorials appeared as did stories deriding the very conservation efforts that had made Philipstown attractive to Roger. He didn't approve of idealistic non-taxpaying organizations with unelected leaders that claimed to be working for the common good.

Lindsley, a stocky, bespectacled youngster, introduced himself to the villagers with a story about an evening forum for candidates for local political office. Because the mayor didn't show up and those in charge kept changing the venue, there was rampant confusion. The candidates and their supporters trailed up and down Main Street for some time before finally finding a home for the debate in a church building. Lindsley thought this hilarious—a bunch of yokels out of a Falstaffian comedy, running around like a flock of turkeys before Thanksgiving—and that was the way he wrote it. Only the shamelessly fanatical in the anti-Ailes camp noted that the mayor, who was supported by the PCNR, was not subjected to Lindsley's humor because he was absent from the evening's proceedings.

When a letter arrived at the paper protesting his smart alecky approach, Lindsley published it but not without a derisive publisher's note. It seemed to me that it was all right, even admirable, to assault the rich, the smug and the powerful but not ordinary folks.

It was an amusing scene, no doubt, that might have found corner space in a metropolitan daily where nobody knows their neighbor but, I thought, this was a local weekly in a village where everybody knew everybody else. The objects of Lindsley's ridicule were struggling under comical circumstances to fulfill their role in local democracy and surely didn't deserve mockery from an outsider who had just arrived on the scene. Brian O'Donnell would have known better.

Shortly after, the paper broke new ground with its first editorial in decades, perhaps ever. It was a right wing diatribe against Barack Obama's bailout and stimulus policies. It tickled Tony because it reminded him of the obscure little Irish newspaper in the days before World War 1 which, in an editorial, warned the Kaiser that the paper had its eye on him. To us, it was even more absurd than the procession up and down Main Street. Now Washington would know that the Putnam County News & Recorder in the village of Cold Spring, N.Y. had its eye on the capital.

I decided that the Country Goose couldn't continue to sell this silly paper with its big headlines about nothing very much. After Beth learned of my decision, she boycotted the store and therefore could no longer return my hugs. She didn't even step inside to give me a one-finger salute. Fair enough. I wouldn't sell her paper so she was fully justified in not spending money with me. In spite of our differences over the role of a village weekly paper, I still liked her. Up to a point, I also liked Joe Lindsley. I once told him that he needed seasoning, that he should buy an old jalopy, drive across the country, grow up and broaden his horizons.

But the worst impact of this new paper was on the serenity of the village. The old PCNR never put its toes into the turbulence of politics or set out to create controversy. But now suddenly the village was divided into two camps. When I dropped the paper, customers either congratulated me or indicated their disapproval of my action. You either supported Roger Ailes and his organ or you despised him and it. Probably I lost some customers and their money but I was not running the store for its meager financial return. For me the attraction was the variety of customers, so many of them interesting or from foreign lands or funny or weird, entertaining in one way or another.

But the village was split as if Roger had taken a chain-saw to it. Candidates for office previously didn't run on the basis of their political beliefs. They ran on their record for competency and their ideas for the future. Now they were either left or right.

People I had known for years without once thinking of their political beliefs revealed themselves as supporters of the right or the left because of the paper which, of course, promoted the views of those on the right. The exception to this non-political philosophy had been Donald Lusk, who had never shied away from making his liberal political leanings clear, but people said, "Oh, that's just Donald being Donald."

None of this was helped when Beth Ailes, immediately before a school budget vote, decided to publish the salaries of teachers in the township. The motive was clear: reject the budget because teachers and administrators were paid too much.

Years before all this, long before the celebrated Leonora/Roger split, I had become curious about the school systems in Cold Spring and neighboring Garrison which assigned a highly paid superintendent individually to both schools even though the little Garrison school, with 280 pupils, only went to eighth grade and paid to send its pupils out of the district for their high school education.

In New York City, a superintendent was responsible for a whole district which included a number of schools, yet in Philipstown both schools needed one. Why? At the least, why couldn't one superintendent oversee the two schools?

I didn't get far. The origin of the system was lost in the haziness of time but, as far as I could tell, it would take action in the state capital, Albany, (vying for the title of most corrupt in the nation) for any changes and it was not the No. 1 issue up there so things stayed as they were.

I had mixed feelings about publishing teachers' salaries. On the one hand, some of their pay came out of taxpayers' pockets and surely the taxpayers, some of them struggling with their own budgets, were entitled to know how their money was being spent. Transparency had become the buzz word. Readers discovered that the Garrison superintendent made more than $160,000 while the principal there pulled in more than $120,000. At Haldane, in Cold Spring, the average salary of teachers was $62,000 which struck me as modest, perhaps too low. A really good teacher, I thought, was worth far more than any multi-millionaire Wall Street shark but a remarkably high-paid superintendent was not even a teacher, just an administrator. And how could you judge the value of a teacher, anyway?

On the other hand, what good did it do? It created mischief, tension, with teachers, most of them with nowhere near a six figure salary, angrily protesting the publication and some taxpayers denouncing them and their union. The teachers played into Beth's hands by holding protest meetings. If their salaries were merely adequate, why object so vocally? As it turned out, the listing didn't stop the budget passing with ease. In fairness, I admit that at least one letter of protest was published in the paper. To me it was a 50-50 proposition so I was almost prepared to give Beth and Roger a pass. Almost.

Then there was the matter of The Area Guide, a bi-annual publication put out by the PCNR, full of locally paid advertisements, telephone numbers and some of the more interesting facts about the area. I had arranged over the years with Metro-North for the visit to Cold Spring of a train-load of "leaf-peepers," eager to enjoy the autumnal colors, The peepers, usually about 400 of them, were always handed a free copy of The Guide on the train to help them shop and find their way around. Before Roger bought the paper, I had paid for an advertisement in the forthcoming little book. But by the time it was published, we had quarreled.

When I called for my usual 400 copies, the girl in the PCNR office, obviously under instructions, refused to let me have them. I was baffled. There were 400 visitors coming, all potential shoppers on Main Street, the perfect captive audience. But this year the paper had decided not to let them have the 400 copies of the Guide. The whole point of it was to tell the visitors a bit about Cold Spring and, more important, help them shop. The Aisles didn't get it. The Guide, which made a profit from advertisements, was not so much for locals, who knew all about the stores and the area, as it was for visitors like the valiant 400.

My usual contact for the Guide at the PCNR was on vacation so I was stumped. But not for long. There wasn't much time but I decided to throw together an eight page version of the Guide, but unlike the Guide specifically aimed at the leaf peepers, so that the 400 would have something to read on the train. It was accompanied by a map showing all the retail businesses, restaurants and local points of interest within walking distance.

I called it The Cold Spring Express, a special edition for Metro-North leaf peepers, October 24, 2009. Designed by Ruth Eisenhower and funded by The Cold Spring Merchants Association, it started off: "Just one hour and 100 years from New York City, our historic riverfront village is a haven from the hustle and bustle of every day life . . ." then went on to promote all the area's attractions. On the second page was a column, written by Tony, but ostensibly by our black Lab, Tara, called Sitting on the Bench. It had been published as an advertisement in O'Donnell's PCNR long before Ailes took over. Tara ruminated about beavers creating litter at Foundry Cove and claimed that when she went swimming in the Hudson she seized unsightly driftwood and brought it to shore to be disposed of.

Next came a list of historic sites worth visiting, then the special events taking place that day. An insert named the Main Street stores offering discounts to the 400. I was quite proud of it. It even had a photograph of a bucolic scene, taken by my friend, Jane Marcy, on the front page and a riverside scene, taken by my friend Ruth, on the back.

The Cold Spring Express was rolling off the presses when I got a phone call at the store from the PCNR. The girl said it had been decided to let me have eighty copies of the Guide. "Useless," I said. "I need at least 400. What, you want five people to share one copy?" She wouldn't budge. It was eighty or nothing. I put the phone down.

A few minutes later, Joe Lindsley stormed into the Goose, smoke and flames issuing from his enraged face. "How dare you," he yelled. "How dare you hang up on one of my employees?" Wow, drama at the Country Goose. He was accompanied by a girl that I took to be my telephone partner. She looked unhappy.

"There was nothing more to be said," I replied. "So I put the phone down. End of story. Now I'm hanging up on you. Please leave my store." Or something like that.

"Never do that again," he growled and stalked off with the girl trailing behind him. Joe, it seemed, could poke fun at the yokels but took a phone hang-up very seriously indeed.

I got the substitute Guide down to Grand Central terminal in time and Metro-North said it was much appreciated by the 400 so the day was saved.

CHAPTER SEVENTEEN

Geographically and politically, Cold Spring was part of the Town of Philipstown. Nobody seemed to think the title was odd, but it seemed comically redundant to me. Anyway, shortly before an election for the supervisor of the township a letter appeared in the PCNR, one which I don't believe Brian O'Donnell would have published because of his rule against personal attacks.

Written by the leader of the local Republican Party, Terry Polhemus, the wife of a well-known Garrison contractor, it raged that a resident named Gordon Stewart was a "washed-up speechwriter" and "puppeteer" who was pulling strings to enable the incumbent supervisor, Richard Shea, to retain his seat. Further, Polhemus denounced Shea as a "marionette" and a "schoolyard bully." Until the letter informed me, I had never realized that Shea was a Democrat because political beliefs had never before been an election issue. He was opposed by a well-financed conservative Republican, Lee Erickson, who enjoyed the backing of Ailes but had declined to appear at two debates with his opponent.

This, I surmised, was the reason for the assault on Gordon Stewart who was not even on the ballot. But Stewart was the creator of a new web site, Philipstown.info, which had offended Roger Aisles mightily by hiring away some of his PCNR staff to write articles competing with news stories in Roger's paper. Because on-line stories could appear almost as soon as written, Philipstown was scooping the PCNR every day on eye-catching incidents like the recovery of a missing cat and the mayor falling off his bike.

I knew Stewart as an occasional shopper in the store, unassuming and polite, but didn't know until later that he was an interesting bloke in an area full of interesting characters. He had been a White House speechwriter for Jimmy Carter, as well as a movie and theater director, an orchestra conductor, a corporate executive and vice president of the American Stock Exchange. Stewart was also a lover and collector of fine art, including a Picasso. For a washed up wretch his pockets must have been full, I thought, because he could afford to launch a not-for-profit on-line newspaper with an office on Main Street and pay a staff of a half dozen or so, without any financial return.

Stewart believed it would be good for his paperless paper and for the township to sponsor a debate between the candidates for supervisor, Shea versus Erickson, including those campaigning for a position on the council. Erickson said, no—without thanks, explaining that he did not believe Stewart, who would act as moderator, would be fair and balanced. He also understandably declined an invitation to a debate sponsored by the League of Women Voters, presumably notorious for its mysterious dislike of Lee Erickson. However, he agreed to appear at a debate arranged by the PCNR, I suppose on the grounds that the Ailes paper was well-known for its avoidance of political bias.

Funded by a handsome donation or two, the Republicans renovated a building across Main Street from the PCNR and opened a headquarters to help them pursue their goals. It would also be handy for celebrating their victory with many a high-five.

When Shea and his Democratic team easily won the election, the headline, "Town to Ailes, Drop Dead" did not appear in the PCNR. But Terry Polhemus, a registered nurse who in her letter had diagnosed Philipstown.info as a "flailing" web site, was by no means down-hearted. She pointed out that although her candidates had lost by 41 per cent to 59 per cent, they had made Philipstown into a two-party town which she seemed to think was a good thing.

Polhemus, a good friend of Beth's, was arrested some months later by State Police at 2 a.m. and accused of drunken driving. Conscious of the demands of journalistic ethics, the PCNR reported the incident, identifying her as the leader of the local GOP, but showed its kindly side by losing the story in a couple of paragraphs deep inside its pages surrounded by advertisements. I wondered if the paper conducted a graveside service for the buried news item. In contrast, Philipstown.info, controlled by the "washed-up speechwriter," ignored the story until Polhemus pleaded guilty to driving while impaired, blaming a mix of alcohol and medication.

I couldn't agree with Polhemus about the value of a two-party village. To me, America was suffering from a surfeit of politics. There wasn't a moment when a political campaign wasn't in progress somewhere, from the President down to the village board member. (It seemed to me that anybody who wanted to take over the White House and thus become the most powerful man or woman on the planet was clinically wacky and therefore should be barred from running for the office)

Almost as soon as a new President was inaugurated, his opponents began plotting and campaigning for the next presidential election. There were elections for (I've probably missed some) governors, for senators, for representatives, for state senators, for state representatives, for city mayors, for county leaders, for district attorneys, for school boards, for town boards, for village boards, for low level judges—which I thought was the most farcical of all.

How on earth could the average voter decide if a lawyer would make a good judge or should retain his seat on the bench? Voters didn't attend court day after day which, it seemed to me, was the only way they could reach a rational conclusion about the views and talents of a candidate. Here's a scenario. A man, very unpopular with fellow townspeople for whatever reason, perhaps a Donald Lusk, is charged with a crime. Out of prejudice against him, together with gossip and rumors, the vast majority of the population has decided he is guilty as charged and made their views known. Privately, the judge disagrees. There is not enough evidence to convict. But his re-election is approaching. Should he rule against the defendant and satisfy the voters? Or should he do the right thing and dismiss the charge, thus endangering his re-election prospects? A judge shouldn't have to take such matters into consideration.

In place of the PCNR, I started following the local news on-line on Philipstown.info. Unlike the PCNR, it held to a policy of straight forward reporting, trying to avoid slanting either to the right or the left. It said it would not publish "vitriolic personal attacks or general ranting" unless the writer was willing to revise his/her tone very substantially. Just as important as this, without the on-line newspaper Ailes' paper would have been the only local voice in Philipstown with no other organ to hold it accountable.

During the town election described earlier, a prominent advertisement attacking the Democratic incumbent, Richard Shea, appeared in the pages of the PCNR Filling half a page, it was unsigned but bore a Maltese cross, often used by fire companies as an emblem, implying the ad came from a fire company. In fact, all of the four volunteer fire companies in the area disavowed sponsorship of the ad. Philipstown.info, holding the newspaper to account, asked why the ad had not been signed and if, in fact, it came from a fire company. A PCNR spokesman was evasive. Transparency was not the buzz word at the Ailes paper. Yes, it knew who had submitted the ad. No, it wouldn't reveal that. Why was it unsigned? It wasn't a letter to the editor, it was a paid advertisement. The spokesman said he would look into the matter, but he suggested that further discussion was unlikely and hung up while his questioner was still pursuing the issue. Such a pity that Joe Lindsley's dislike of people hanging up telephones had not taken root at the PCNR.

Philipstown.info contacted a number of volunteer firemen, many of them vocally dismayed that somebody had pretended to speak for them in this manner. Supervisor Shea suggested that the attack ad might well backfire, with some of the firemen voting for him as a result. A number of them had called him, he said, even those who didn't support him, expressing their disgust.

Reporting all this, Philipstown dot info expressed sadness that so many of its letters were hostile. Better to present reasoned argument. Then it turned the screw on the PCNR a little more by offering a free advertising section to its readers.

Stewart, however, emphasized whenever asked that he had no ambition to damage or destroy the PCNR. He merely wanted to give readers interested in local news an alternative. I doubt that Roger, deprived of owning the sole megaphone in Philipstown, accepted that.

Together with Tony, I was a little surprised that Roger Ailes' take-over of a village weekly, as well as an ailing one he bought on the other side of the county, had aroused no interest in daily papers or magazines. Here was a powerful, controversial figure on the national scene, like him or not, who was focusing on an upstate area of no more than ten thousand people when his national TV audience ran to millions. Yet, except for the occasional glancing reference, his sortie into rusticity was ignored.

That changed when a staff writer for the New Yorker magazine, living in Westchester County, talked to a newly-arrived neighbor who had been living in Cold Spring before her move south. The writer's curiosity was aroused by what the neighbor said and he decided to have a look at the situation. The neighbor had suggested he call me to start his inquiries, which he did. He told me he was planning a visit to Cold Spring to find out what was going on. He sounded like a nice bloke so I agreed to help in any way I could. Checking on his background, I found he had worked for the Los Angeles Times, the New York Times and now the New Yorker so it could be assumed he was filled to the brim with integrity. His magazine, which rarely competed with the National Enquirer, was respected and trusted by its readers. In fact, it was well-known that the New Yorker was so fixated on assuring accuracy that it employed fact-checkers to follow up on the work of its writers.

When he arrived at the store, introducing himself as Peter Boyer, I suggested, as fellow journalists, he should talk to Tony. Sure, he said, he'd be in the Silver Spoon restaurant and bar across the street. On his arrival, Tony was surprised to find the visiting writer sitting at the bar with the demon editor of Main Street, Joe Lindsley. In casual conversation, Tony made the mistake of expressing his aversion to the South where, as an intruding reporter from the North, he had experienced threats and serious unfriendliness from whites while covering Martin Luther King Jr., and the civil rights struggles in Mississippi and Alabama. As Lindsley, also a Southern good ol' boy, sat listening, smiling like the cat from Cheshire, our visitor said he was from Mississippi and defended his roots by telling the story of how friendly Southerners had gone out of their way to help him when his car broke down. Yes, well, he was a native son of the South and he was white.

When the three left the bar—surprisingly little had been said about Ailes, the PCNR or Philipstown—. Tony competed with Southern hospitality by helping Boyle find his way into the hills for an appointment at the home of Gordon Stewart. The creator of Philipstown.info was to become a central figure in the New Yorker story.

In his piece, brightened by a full-page photograph of a glamorized Beth, the reporter quoted Tony as saying that on Main Street I was "Gossip Central—Radio Leonora." Cheeky Tony, but there was some truth to it. One day, three smartly dressed, affluent-looking, Spanish-speaking ladies came into the store and spent freely. Two spoke English and translated for the third. Shortly thereafter, Connie at a store, Country Touch, down the street, telephoned me to ask, "Have you seen three Spanish ladies in your store? One of them left her purse on my counter and there's nearly a thousand dollars in it."

I went out to the street to see if the three were in view. Down the street, Connie was doing the same thing. No sight of them. We shrugged. A bit later, I got a call from one of the three asking about her missing purse. She was at Boscobel, the restored mansion a mile or so outside Cold Spring. When she told the people there that she had lost her purse, probably on Main Street, they told her to call me. "Leonora will know if anybody has found it," they said. The woman did in fact call me and I put her in touch with Connie. The trio rewarded Connie by spending 40 more dollars in her store. Happy ending because of Gossip Central. So there, Tony.

Evidently the New Yorker writer and Lindsley, sharing a Southern background, had bonded because in the story that was published Boyer called the young editor "smart," "combative," "intensely competitive," with "an aggressive news instinct," seeming to be "a younger version of Ailes," the last description later causing some smirks around Cold Spring. The New Yorker called the Ailes version of the PCNR "a manifest improvement" over the O'Donnell paper. Hah!

And, taking a rosy view of developments, he ended with the thought that Ailes and Stewart had produced a kind of symbiosis, beneficial to the community. "Many places a thousand times larger are served by only a single newspaper," he wrote, "Philipstown now has two, each distinctly better than what was there before." Pollyanna rides again. If I display a trace of hostility towards the New Yorker it may be because I don't understand most of their mysteriously opaque cartoons. It's probably my fault, my dimness a result of my truncated education or the trauma caused by the sight of my father's bandaged head. Roger, however, must have enjoyed the tone of the article with its omissions because later he hired the writer as editor-at-large, whatever that is, for Fox News.

I should add that unfortunately the article appeared before the town election campaign ran its course, with all the dubious tactics on display. But I try to be gracious so I'll excuse the New Yorker for its stumble.

Now I had been a magazine publisher and a book editor of sorts but I was not a journalist. Even so there was something else in the New Yorker piece that caught my attention. It popped up when the reporter was interviewing Roger.

I'm sorry to say that Roger, what a rascal, misled his questioner as Roger denigrated one of his favorite targets, a non-profit conservation outfit called Open Spaces. Sadly, the New Yorker allowed him to get away with it. The issue being discussed was a riverside meadow of about a half dozen acres on the western edge of the village, offering a splendid view across the Hudson of Storm King. Called Dockside, it was used by villagers for strolling, playing Frisbee, admiring Storm King, picnics and walking their pets. At the very far end, occupying a fraction of the total space, stood a restaurant in a terrible state of repair.

The New Yorker's Boyer reported it was on Main Street, which it was not. "In 1999," the reporter wrote, "the property was acquired by the Open Space Institute, the restaurant subsequently closed and the building was demolished. A 'passive use' open area, called Dockside Park, now occupies the lot."

Missing from this were some facts. The tumble-down restaurant was bulldozed before it could collapse under its own disintegrating weight. It would have cost thousands of dollars to rehabilitate it and make it safe for public use. The disappearance of the restaurant made no difference whatsoever to the use of the meadow which had always been available to the public for leisure pursuits.

But this is what Roger, mourning the loss of the restaurant, told the New Yorker: "The 'greater good' obviously could not be served by people sitting down there watching the river go by, having a beer or a hamburger. So now we have an entire field of dog crap. And that's what's in the greater good, that we're down there trying not to step in dog crap because everybody in town walks their dog down there. Now the dog has a pretty good view of the river from there. But the dog cannot get a beer. So I would argue that the greater good has not been served."

Wow, he sounded like one of his choleric TV clowns who are constantly proving that a lie travels around the world before truth gets its pants on. Where do I start? First, a touch of irony. I walked our dog, Tara, at the park every morning and I always carried a plastic bag to scoop up her droppings. So did most of the morning dog squad. On one occasion, I reprimanded a villager for not cleaning up after his dog and he told me to fuck off. I knew him and I knew he was an Ailes supporter. Lovely.

To say that you had to avoid stepping in "dog crap" all over the meadow was, putting it mildly, incorrect. Sure, there's the occasional evidence of anti-social behavior by pet-owners like Roger's fan, but the bulk of any droppings came from a flock of squawking Canada geese which congregated for some reason near the site of the vanished restaurant. Perhaps Roger hadn't studied the difference between various types of . . . . Oh, that's enough of that.

Why all these dogs only appeared at Dockside after the distant restaurant had gone, naughty Roger did not explain. It was so confusing. Was Roger suggesting that dogs should be given a beer while enjoying the view of the Hudson?

In accord with the New Yorker policy, a fact checker phoned Tony and me to make sure our quotes were accurate. He sounded like a nice young man and he kindly altered a few words in the story to avoid embarrassing a villager we had mentioned. But it seemed he wasn't given the task of checking on the truth of assertions in the story. Barring that, I think the New Yorker should have sent its reporter to investigate the bowel movements at Dockside of Cold Spring's dogs.

Some weeks after the magazine article appeared, there was a strange development involving Roger, Beth, Joe Lindsley and, my goodness, espionage. An article in the on-line gossip web site, Gawker, said that all had not been serene behind the handsome façade of the PCNR. In fact, hostility had been bubbling like boiling water between the trio. The article might have been dismissed as mere malicious scuttlebutt but it was given authority by a statement issued by, of all people, Beth.

To put the matter in context, we have to go back to the time when Roger took over the weekly and addressed the staff he had inherited. According to Michael Turton, one of the PCNR reporters who later emigrated to Philipstown.info, Roger said they could all keep their jobs. But, Turton told the New Yorker, there was a proviso. They must never ever bad-mouth their employer, namely Roger. Indeed I knew from acquaintances that Roger was so sensitive that he would accuse people, innocent as angels, of gossiping about him and his activities, an unforgivable offense.

Here's what Gawker disclosed under the headline: Roger Ailes Caught Spying on the Reporters at his Small Town Newspaper. Gawker claimed that editor Lindsley had resigned from the PCNR before he was interviewed a month or so later by the New Yorker magazine. If Lindsley mentioned that little detail to his interviewer it did not appear in the New Yorker which struck me as strange since the two Southerners had bonded so well. However, Lindsley agreed to fulfill his editorial duties for another three months presumably until his successor could be found.

Gawker said the reason for the rift was that Roger accused Lindsley and two of his reporters of "badmouthing" him and Beth during their lunch breaks. Because Roger said he knew which restaurant they frequented, the trio concluded they had been followed. Lindsley cut his transition period short and quit outright along with the two reporters.

"After Lindsley quit for good, things got weirder," Gawker said. "He was driving to a deli in Cold Spring for lunch . . . when he noticed a black Lincoln Navigator that seemed to be following him. Lindsley drove aimlessly for a while to make sure he was being followed and the Navigator stayed with him. Then he got a look at the driver, who was a News Corporation security staffer"—a goon in Gawker's jargon—"that Lindsley happened to know socially." When Lindsley contacted the bodyguard to question what was going on, the security man said he was following him at Roger's direction.

Gawker added that Lindsley had been treated as a member of the Ailes family, escorting Beth to Sunday church services in Roger's absence and, on Roger's instructions, rushing to the Ailes compound to deal with a suspected break-in which turned out to be a false alarm.

There was a claim that Beth had once joked to Lindsley that after dear Roger died he would have to take on her husband's "special responsibilities." Wasn't it the New Yorker that had described Lindsley as "a younger version of Ailes"?

Now all this could be taken with rock-sized lump of salt except that Beth issued a statement flatly denying that there was any truth in Gawker's story. But then she went on, "The paper hoped for Joe's success in spite of his personal habits and lack of performance which included getting the weekly editions out late and over budget for three months. There's a sad disconnect between his claims of undying gratitude and his current state of agitation."

To me, that burst of hostility supported Gawker's story in a way that almost nothing else could have done. Wouldn't it have been much wiser for Beth to have simply heaped praise on Joe Lindsley as a marvelous worker and friend whose resignation was much regretted at PCNR and who would be terribly missed as he went on to exciting new ventures? And, without any sign of frostiness between them, left it at that?

Lefties, I believed, were too simplistic when they labeled Roger an arch ogre from the dark side. I'm sure he has many splendid characteristics, including a soft heart concealed behind his grimly smiling exterior. A kinder story going the rounds was that while shopping at a Main Street store he chatted to the owner and discovered the store was in financial trouble. Roger, it seems, immediately awarded the owner a $5,000 loan to help him out. Bravissimo! I don't know if the loan was ever repaid but I expect that modest Roger, behind the scenes, has engaged in other philanthropy. And he had a sense of humor. Before they stopped speaking to each other, he told Gordon, "Dammit, Stewart, I'm sick and tired of making you famous."

Another admirable aspect of Roger, up to a point, was Beth Ailes. I noted that in the New Yorker article she described shopping in the local stores (not mine, of course) where sometimes, she said, she encountered hostility. She could have avoided such unpleasantness by sending a lackey to do her shopping but, no, she defied her enemies by putting on her lipstick and going to the supermarket and drug store like any other Cold Spring housewife. Good for her. Gordon, however, wouldn't agree with my encomium. He complained that Beth had brazenly lied when she declared that a letter from an aggrieved woman, prominent in Philipstown, had been received too late for inclusion in her paper. In fact, it was never published.

CHAPTER EIGHTEEN

As time went by, the number of stories about Roger and Beth and their demands for control of everything in sight inevitably mounted in the village. Some rumors were too unbelievable to be believable. Such a one was my favorite. It concerned Boscobel, the restored mansion lying at the base of the hill owned by Roger. The mansion and some of its grounds were plainly visible, part of the splendid up-river view from Roger's sprawling compound.

Every summer a large tent was erected at Boscobel for audiences attending the popular annual Shakespeare festival. It was shielded from Roger's sight by trees so it was not an issue. But one day a much smaller white tent was erected closer to the mansion presumably for a wedding or some sort of celebration. Now there was a problem because Roger could see it.

The story going around claimed that he complained that it was ruining his wonderful and expensive view and something had to be done. It was. Boscobel, conscious of Roger's generosity to the area, moved the little tent until it was out of Roger's sight.

Another story showed that Roger was not an enemy of all trees so long as they were in the right place. According to the gossip, a team of landscapers was, in the absence of the Ailes family, working on the grounds of the compound. They were planting a tree when the boss's cell phone rang. It was the absent Beth. "No, no," she said. "That's not where I want the tree. I insist that you move it." She directed them to the correct site. The landscapers were puzzled until they realized that the many security cameras on the grounds had captured them at work. Beth had been watching them from wherever she was and called to correct the tree planting. Obviously another false rumor. Altogether though, these unlikely stories were most entertaining.

One story turned out to be entirely accurate, however. It was that Gordon Stewart, Jimmy Carter's speechwriter and creator of the on-line Philipstown.info who said he didn't want to damage the PCNR, was launching a free weekly newspaper with paid advertisements called The Paper in direct competition with Roger's weekly. Immediately I placed an advertisement for the Goose in the Paper and ordered a bunch of them to put in the shopping bags and baskets of my customers.

Even before the appearance of The Paper, a handsome, sprightly tabloid in color, both Roger and his new editor/columnist/enforcer were separately on the phone to Stewart having a good rant about liberal conspiracies. They suggested, reported Stewart, that Facebook co-founder Chris Hughes, a Democrat who had an estate in the Garrison hills, was financing The Paper. Still in his 20s, Hughes had used his networking skills to help elect Barack Obama in his first campaign for the White House. Or was it the hated non-profit Hudson Valley Land Trust? Or the local Democratic politicians?. "No," said Stewart. "I'm financing it on my own."

Stewart said that Roger kept calling him. After the second one, Stewart declared that there was nothing more to be said and put down the phone. Ailes called again, this time yelling, "You have a mental health problem. You need a psychiatrist." Stewart hung up. A fourth call came from Roger and this time, Stewart said with some satisfaction he just let it ring.

More interesting than this pouting by the Fox boss was Roger's disclosure to Stewart that he had passed ownership of the PCNR to Beth. Say what you like, Roger was a generous husband. But if he was no longer the owner then what right did he have to yell at her competitors? Did he no longer believe in the freedom to compete, the icon of his beloved right wing, the very root of capitalism? I certainly thought that Rupert Murdoch should be told that Roger had strayed out of the fold.

In eager pursuit of the truth or falsity of all these rumors, I asked my rabid dog researcher, Tony, to contact Roger for his response. Tony wrote, requesting an interview. A week or two later, Roger took time from his duties to reply with a polite letter which turned down the request and included a little sting. "Unfortunately," he wrote, "I already know your opinion of me since it's pretty much spread around town and I see no upside to the interview." Tony was a tad bewildered by this because he had never talked to Roger beyond an exchanged "Hello" once when they were introduced to each other on Main Street and shook hands before parting. That was it. We hoped that Roger had not been listening to village gossip which, of course, is notoriously unreliable.

Roger went on to say that he was writing his own book in which Cold Spring and some of its residents would be discussed. He added that his book would be published by HarperCollins. It occurred to me that since HarperCollins was controlled by his boss, Rupert Murdoch, it would be a self-published work. (HarperCollins published Tony's latest book, deploying distressing incompetence. So good luck with that, Roger.} His note ended with him wishing Tony the best in the future. How sweet.

Gordon Stewart psycho-analyzed Roger's letter and decided it was classic passive-aggressive. On the one hand, Roger was trying to be gentlemanly, but at the same time he couldn't resist introducing a blunt instrument. No upside? "He's a thug," said Gordon. "He would have done better to have ignored the request or said he didn't have the time."

Comedy turned into farce when a writer, Gabriel Sherman, who was putting together a book about Roger, disclosed that his subscription to the PCNR had been cancelled. When he called to ask why, the editor said that because of his forthcoming book, "We do not desire to have a relationship with you." Sherman's wife then tried to subscribe but was also rejected as unfit to be a reader.

I thought of testing my relationship with PCNR by applying for a subscription but decided it would be too depressing if they turned me down because I didn't meet the high standards required of all readers of the Putnam County News and Recorder.

Those standards, it turned out, also applied to advertisers. Representatives of organizations like the Democratic Party and the competing Philipstown.info, keen to place ads in the paper, were barred from its pristine pages. A more generous side was displayed, though, when some villagers were offered free subscriptions to the paper. Only the cynical suggested that was because the PCNR circulation was not doing what it was supposed to do.

Talking to the New Yorker earlier about the new Philipstown.info, Roger said he had lunched with Stewart who told him that he (Stewart) was financing Philipstown from his own funds. "He's going to get very tired of doing that," Roger said dismissively. It sounded as though Roger had made the mistake of under-estimating how full Stewart's pockets were. If I were nouveau riche and had millions of dollars rolling in, I might be inclined to think that I was surrounded by country bumpkins who were paupers compared to me. In fact, there was a lot of money and not many food stamps in the hills surrounding Cold Spring, belonging to people who shied away from publicity.

The owner of Subway Sandwiches, a global franchise, applied for membership of the local Fish and Game Club and, after he mentioned his connection with Subway, was asked which outlet he ran.

"All of them," he replied. Or so the story went.

Facebook plutocrat Chris Hughes and his partner Sean Eldridge, also in his 20s, a Democratic activist who had considered running for Congress, were reported by Forbes magazine to be worth a total of around $700 million. Then there was Patty Hearst, whose sprawling Garrison estate overlooked the Hudson. And there was a pack of Wall Street investment bankers surely praying every night that they would not attract the attention of a prosecutor or grand jury.

I was happy to see that, like O'Donnell's old PCNR, the Paper took no ranting political position although in its first edition it had a comprehensive, unbiased story about the five Democrats competing to take on Republican Rep. Nan Heyworth in the next election. It was a story that I doubt Roger would have found acceptable. (Heyworth lost.)

.Now Philipstown had two print newspapers and an on-line news source. The PCNR also had a news web site although nobody took much notice of that. My goodness, a newspaper war in little Cold Spring. It was doubtful that any other area in the country was to be covered so intensely.

In Cold Spring, there was plenty to cover. At the top of the list was the riveting question: Should Cold Spring (A Timeless Town) play host to a Dunkin Donuts? If the answer was yes, would it be followed by McDonalds, Burger King, Taco Bell and all the rest of the coast-to-coast franchises that had made American towns look identical? Was that what Victorian-era Cold Spring wanted?

The question was raised by Kenny Elmes, a well-known local figure who owned a Citgo gas pump business and repair garage on Route 9-D which ran through the center of the village. Kenny had suffered terrible injuries in a motor cycle accident and lost a leg which together with other health problems, he said, made it impossible for him to work as a mechanic as he used to before the crash. This meant that he could no longer prosper from his gas station. Therefore, he proposed that while the pumps would continue to operate he wanted to turn the repair bays of the garage into a Dunkin Donuts drive-through. He wouldn't run the donut shop but he had the people who would and their rent would enable him to survive.

The usual suspects gathered their forces. The vanished editor of the PCNR, Joe Lindsley, had been succeeded by a less-fiery, more circumspect and older editor, Douglas Cunningham, who sometimes published a column of his views called "Cunningham's Corner." Whether he was expected to escort Beth to church, I, not a churchgoer, did not know. But his views happened to coincide with those of Roger Ailes. Fancy that. Cunningham did not outright endorse the establishment of a Dunkin Donuts but, always in favor of business development, he leaned Kenny's way almost to the horizontal by casting a disapproving eye at its opponents. In a phrase that Lindsley would have applauded, he called them "apoplectic." Unfortunately, he looked more like an assistant bank manager than a hard fisted newspaperman.

Other supporters declared there were already chain businesses in Cold Spring, including a Drug World and Foodtown, which belonged to a small group of supermarkets, so there would be nothing unusual about a Dunkin Donuts joining them. In truth, the difference was that these were not franchises but were owned and operated by the chains. I suppose the Dunkin supporters could have added the national chain of Post Offices and the two bank branches which had headquarters elsewhere.

In the opposing trenches were fighters for Cold Spring's historical eminence who argued that the donut store would be "out of character" and would cause traffic jams around Kenny's place. One of their most effective arguments was the simple one that Kenny didn't even live in Cold Spring. He would be able to retreat to his residence miles away in East Fishkill, leaving in his wake the urban chaos he had created in Cold Spring.

Called on to make a decision, the village planning board did what boards almost always do. It delayed its verdict and hoped that the problem would go away. In the meantime, the board held a meeting for public comments. There was something of a journalistic breakthrough when a reporter for the PCNR, Tim Greco, rose to throw his support behind the establishment of the Dunkin Donuts. He said he was taking off his reporter's hat so that he could speak freely. The busy Mr. Greco, who was also pastor of a church in neighboring Nelsonville, then put his reporter's hat back on and chronicled the meeting with a story that said most of those attending the meeting supported his view. Conflict of interest? Nah.

As for me, I decided I couldn't go far wrong if I automatically opposed the views of Roger's newspaper in any debate about the future of Cold Spring or, indeed, anything else. So that's what I did. An anti-Dunkin Donuts graphic went on the door of the Goose. Kenny sent a mutual friend to the store to ask me very politely if I would take it down. Equally politely, I said I wouldn't. After months and months, the board gave Kenny a green light. Perhaps I should have put up a bigger sign. Immediately an argument about the size of the Dunkin Donuts sign broke out. A very argumentative village, Cold Spring.

But I had a more serious personal fight confronting me. This villain was called Amazon and its tentacles had reached into my store and Main Street shops across America. For me, it began when a woman shopper came into the Goose and began to take photographs of items on the shelves. I didn't say anything but later learned what she was doing. She was using a barcode app on her phone to compare prices. The deal Amazon was offering at that time was: If you see something you like in a store, check the price with ours, order from us and we will give you a further discount. To combat these tactics I removed all barcodes from my merchandize so customers can no longer compare prices.

But still shoppers came with their little gizmos, taking pictures of my stock before zapping into the monstrous Amazon for a better deal. When I asked the shoppers what they were doing, they looked guilty, muttered some nonsense or denied they were taking photographs. I told them to put their cute little cameras away.

Amazon was using the Goose and millions of bricks and mortar stores around the country as a showcase. The one thing on-line outfits couldn't offer customers was the ability to touch and closely examine an item. But if shoppers could examine something in a store and then go to Amazon, the problem was solved.

The mantra was that small businesses like mine—and you couldn't get much smaller than mine—were the heart and soul of the American economy. I came across an ad placed in the New York Times by Citi Bank. It read: "This week, Citi celebrates National Small Business Week. Just like last week. And the week before that. Small business owners are the backbone of our economy, and we proudly stand behind them." Hah!

If the small business was so important, why did Congress ditch the Main Street Fairness Act which would have tackled the problem of Amazon and other on-line stores failing to pay taxes like small businesses had to and as a result being able to offer discounts? Maybe it had something to do with the Amazon lobbyists who besieged Washington law makers in opposition to the bill and with Amazon's political action committee which spent $214,000 to promote its cause during the 2010 election cycle.

Amazon said that their customers should declare their purchases when they did their personal taxes and pay the sales tax themselves. Again, hah!

Large manufacturers and retailers recognized that they, too, were being damaged and launched their own campaigns against Amazon, some manufacturers telling the monster that they would sell only to the brick and mortar stores that had supported them for decades. I just wanted to add my squeak of protest to their roars.

One small store on Main Street proved it could survive against the threat of a national colossus. C & E Paints, a family operation, sold everything from pots of paint to tiny screws and sandpaper. When Home Depot opened a hug emporium 20-minutes away from Cold Spring disaster loomed. But C & E offered personal, friendly service and they knew their customers from the many years they had been in business. To save a few dollars, a construction or repair guy in Philipstown who suddenly needed a wrench for a job could spend an hour driving to Home Depot, wandering their aisles and driving back. Or they could pop round to C & E Paints where Sue would produce what they wanted in seconds and let them put it on the tab as well as supplying a chat. Many chose the local store. Well done, C & E Paints.

CHAPTER NINETEEN

For a moment, let's put aside my Paraguay and Hungary approach to America. It turned out that I was by no means alone in my doubts about the value of the U.S. Constitution. Historians report that back in the 1700s the authors of "The Federalist Papers" mocked the "imbecility" of the political system set up by the Articles of Confederation. Even to me, that sounded a little too harsh. After all, the founding fathers were doing their best without being able to foresee the enormous cultural and political changes that would develop in America.

The complaint came to my attention through an article in the New York Times by Sanford Levinson, a professor of law and government at the University of Texas, (and we know the work of professors must never be questioned} who quoted the scorching opinion of the writers of "The Federalist Papers" and went on to designate Article V of the constitution as its worst single section because, the professor pointed out, it made amendments to bring it into the modern world nearly impossible. Darned right. My suggestion for an amendment: "No national political campaign may last more than a calendar month." Who could be against that? Well, I suppose the lobbying and political adviser industry, together with TV advertising managers, might take offense.

Further, too often the admirers of the Constitution injected a whiff of sanctity into the document as though God had guided the writers when, in fact, they clearly were as fallible as anybody. The veneration of the document, I thought, was like a yachtsman sailing for home port without taking into account changing circumstances like the wind, the waves, the tide and essential repairs to the rigging.

How could Americans revere a document that allowed states to decide if women, blacks, men without property, should be allowed to vote? How unfortunate that it took 150 years for the Constitution to be amended to give women the vote and another 45 for blacks in the South to be allowed to enter the voting booth.

Then there was the matter of the Supreme Court which, although accountable to nobody, had as much if not more power than the President and the Congress. Members could do absurd things like awarding an election to a presidential candidate (George W. Bush, 2000) when the majority of voters across the country had made it clear they preferred his opponent. Calling themselves The Supremes, if it wasn't already taken, they could form a chorus line and dance and sing as they made their way to the bench and nobody could say them nay. Indeed the assembly of obsequious lawyers might well cheer them on. I would love to see that. Oh, I couldn't. No cameras in court.

To my mind, equally ridiculous was the stipulation that, with certain exceptions, a presidential candidate had to have been born in America. What was the point? If immigrants gave birth to a child a week before arriving in the States, why, then the child would be barred however brilliant a leader. If a week later when they had landed they produced a child, however stupid, the rule wouldn't apply. Clearly it's discrimination.

Get rid of that nonsensical rule and not only would you abandon the silliness. You would also make sure that a publicity-seeking chump like Donald Trump—aka Mr. Toad of Toad Hall—couldn't use it to bloviate on our TV screens to the detriment of the common good.

These complaints, I thought, were legitimate, if irritating to Americans, but only a small part of the story. A country consisted of the land and its people, not their sometimes foolish laws. It was a land where voters had selected an African-American for their President, not because he was black but because he was the better man. And I liked, even loved, many of the Americans I had encountered. There was Frank, the flight instructor who saved my life. Of course, he saved his own, which was nice. There was Felix, our smiling doorman on 58th Street in Manhattan who thirty years after we left his building still sent us Christmas cards every year. In Woodstock, there were Nestor Bryant and Schultzy. There was Butch Harris in Cold Spring. There were film-maker Bob Jiras, and lovely Brigga and courageous Homer Bigart and cranky Donald Lusk and in Cold Spring so many others like Diane and Curt (not forgetting guide dog Harry), Mos and Pos, Ron and Jane of The Dog Squad, Dave Cooke of the CSMA, Sheila, Dan and Fred—even including Insulter-in-Chief David Duffy—who showed me nothing but kindness. I can't remember ever being treated as an alien, an outsider who didn't belong in the village with the right to make my opinions known.

To me, they and the spectacular land are America, One day, perhaps, America will get it right as it so often does more than any other country, except heavenly Wales. So I forgive all the faults which is extremely gracious of me. It was Winston Churchill, nobody more English yet half American, who said, "You can always count on Americans to do the right thing—after they've tried everything else." So we'll have to wait. In the meantime, my bonds with my home country, however much they loosen, remain. Once a year, I fly to London, but it's mainly to see Rob and his wife, Cathrine, and to spoil their children. It's lovely to be in the U.K. but my pulse still quickens when I land back at JFK.

I'm here and I'm content. I am at home.